C000262038

FF

BELGIUM & THE NETHERLANDS

contents

Map pages	II
Map symbols	III
Route planner	IV
Distance chart	1
Road atlas	2-43
Index and city environs plans	44-60

Amsterdam	44	Luxembourg	52
Brussel/Bruxelles	46	Paris	54-55

3rd edition April 2002
1st edition February 1996

© Automobile Association Developments Limited 2002

 **Ordnance Survey**® This product includes mapping data licensed from Ordnance Survey® with the permission of the Controller of Her Majesty's Stationery Office. © Crown copyright 2002. All rights reserved. Licence number 399221.

Published by AA Publishing (a trading name of Automobile Association Developments Limited, whose registered office is Millstream, Maidenhead Road, Windsor, Berkshire, SL4 5GD. Registered number 1878835).

Mapping produced by the Cartographic Department of The Automobile Association. This atlas has been compiled and produced from the Automaps database utilising electronic and computer technology (A01160).

ISBN 0 7495 3345 5

A CIP catalogue for this book is available from The British Library.

Printed by Scotprint.

map pages

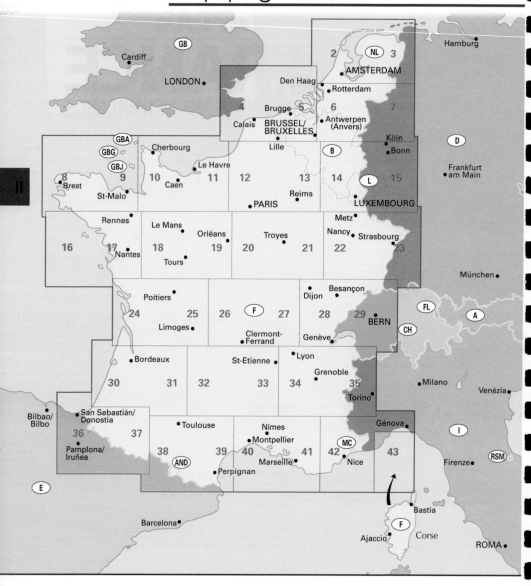

A Austria	**F** France	**GBA** Alderney
AND Andorra	**FL** Liechtenstein	**GBG** Guernsey
B Belgium	**GB** United Kingdom of Great Britain and Northern Ireland	**GBJ** Jersey
CH Switzerland		**I** Italy
D Germany		**L** Luxembourg
E Spain		

MC Monaco	
NL Netherlands	
RSM San Marino	

map symbols

Toll motorways

A55 / E55	Dual carriageway with road numbers
	Single carriageway
⊙	Interchange
⊙	Restricted interchange
Ⓢ	Service area
▪▪▪▪▪▪	Under construction

Non-toll motorways

A55 / E55	Dual carriageway with road numbers
	Single carriageway
⊙	Interchange
⊙	Restricted interchange
Ⓢ	Service area
▪▪▪▪▪▪	Under construction

National roads

SS45	Dual carriageway with road number
	Single carriageway

Regional roads

SS45	Dual carriageway with road number
	Single carriageway

Local roads

SS453	Dual carriageway with road number
	Single carriageway
D28	Minor road with road number

33	Page overlap and number

Symbols

E55 E55	European international network numbers
⊨=====⊣	Motorway in tunnel
⊨=====⊣	Road in tunnel
▬▬▬▬▬▬	Road under construction
⌂	Toll point
▼ 24 ▼	Distances in kilometres
⟩⟩	Gradient 14% and over
⟩	Gradient 6%-13%
10-6 Furkapass 2431	Mountain pass with closure period
3970	Spot height (metres)
▲ EIGER	
⛴	Ferry route (all year)
⛴	Hovercraft (all year)
✈	Airport (International)
+++++++++	Car transporter (rail)
	Mountain railway
🏁	Motor racing circuit
☀ ☀	Viewpoint (180° or 360°)
	Urban area
⊙	Town location
	Canal
	Wooded area

Boundaries

▪▬·▬·▬▪	International
+ · + · + · + ·	National
– – – – –	Unrecognised international
═⊗═	Restricted frontier crossing

scale

1:1 000 000

10 kilometres : 1 centimetre

16 miles : 1 inch

IV

This is a distance chart (triangular matrix) listing road distances in kilometres between European cities. Each city label heads a diagonal; the numbers in each row give distances from that row's origin city to the cities listed along the diagonals. Reading the chart: the labels (top to bottom) are the row origins, and the columns correspond to the same cities in order.

Brugge - Rotterdam = 181km

City	Amsterdam (NL)	Andorra la Vella (AND)	Antwerpen (B)	Arnhem (NL)	Barcelona (E)	Bern (CH)	Bonn (D)	Bordeaux (F)	Brest (F)	Brugge (B)	Brussel/Bruxelles (B)	Calais (F)	Cherbourg (F)	Clermont-Ferrand (F)	Den Haag (NL)	Dijon (F)	Genève (CH)	Groningen (NL)	Le Havre (F)	Le Mans (F)	Liège (B)	Limoges (F)	Luxembourg (L)	Lyon (F)	Marseille (F)	Milano (I)	Nantes (F)	Nice (F)	Oostende (B)	Orléans (F)	Paris (F)	Perpignan (F)	Reims (F)	Rotterdam (NL)	San Sebastián/Donostia (E)	St-Malo (F)	Strasbourg (F)	Toulouse (F)	Tours (F)
Andorra la Vella (AND)	1407																																						
Antwerpen (B)	156	1248																																					
Arnhem (NL)	104	1407	157																																				
Barcelona (E)	1582	189	1425	1532																																			
Bern (CH)	843	900	728	747	909																																		
Bonn (D)	289	1367	225	193	1376	580																																	
Bordeaux (F)	1105	430	946	1105	630	874	1087																																
Brest (F)	1063	1056	904	1063	1256	1141	1045	630																															
Brugge (B)	249	1190	93	250	1422	803	337	888	842																														
Brussel/Bruxelles (B)	203	1194	46	204	1382	689	229	892	850	103																													
Calais (F)	367	1181	208	368	1413	878	434	879	722	122	200																												
Cherbourg (F)	799	1083	640	799	1283	949	781	657	400	578	586	458																											
Clermont-Ferrand (F)	949	568	790	950	624	515	886	355	804	732	736	723	728																										
Den Haag (NL)	63	1383	132	125	1558	867	310	1081	1039	215	179	343	775	925																									
Dijon (F)	743	830	586	692	840	268	537	763	868	583	543	574	676	349	719																								
Genève (CH)	997	755	772	901	764	157	731	716	1092	769	729	760	900	357	905	197																							
Groningen (NL)	180	1558	307	168	1694	910	354	1256	1214	400	354	518	950	1100	238	855	1065																						
Le Havre (F)	614	1033	455	615	1193	797	597	655	473	394	401	274	209	576	590	524	748	765																					
Le Mans (F)	727	859	568	727	1059	748	709	433	402	510	514	419	276	403	703	476	700	878	213																				
Liège (B)	240	1254	119	197	1338	645	138	952	910	203	95	301	646	797	248	499	685	365	462	574																			
Limoges (F)	921	492	762	922	692	671	904	222	609	704	708	695	590	177	897	436	514	1072	548	305	769																		
Luxembourg (L)	415	1164	258	362	1173	480	207	952	967	329	215	417	734	683	391	334	520	525	568	574	171	769																	
Lyon (F)	938	619	781	888	629	305	733	538	1020	778	738	769	828	179	914	196	148	1051	676	628	695	429	530																
Marseille (F)	1271	488	1114	1221	498	598	1066	650	1276	1111	1071	1102	1161	480	1247	529	453	1384	1009	861	1028	712	863	318															
Milano (I)	1097	964	982	1001	973	382	831	1126	1457	1053	939	1206	1265	626	1118	633	389	1161	1113	1065	896	876	731	438	522														
Nantes (F)	907	756	748	907	956	928	889	330	300	690	694	599	317	483	883	656	880	1058	390	185	754	309	754	648	976	1095													
Nice (F)	1427	646	1270	1349	656	604	1179	808	1434	1267	1227	1258	1317	636	1403	636	585	1509	1165	1025	1183	870	1018	473	205	317	1134												
Oostende (B)	281	1201	122	282	1434	814	348	899	819	36	114	99	555	744	257	594	781	432	371	521	215	716	340	790	1123	1068	701	1278											
Orléans (F)	656	760	497	656	920	638	459	549	439	443	430	434	303	632	300	524	807	282	156	503	275	503	452	769	915	305	924	450										
Paris (F)	520	884	361	521	1043	584	503	582	596	303	307	294	356	426	496	312	536	671	204	204	368	398	379	464	797	901	384	952	315	133									
Perpignan (F)	1402	171	1245	1351	184	729	1196	449	1075	1242	1202	1233	1102	444	1378	659	584	1514	1012	879	1158	511	993	448	317	793	775	475	1253	739	863								
Reims (F)	479	1020	322	479	1138	603	440	718	732	287	274	278	499	562	455	298	485	630	347	340	267	534	237	494	827	931	520	982	298	269	144	957							
Rotterdam (NL)	82	1351	101	117	1526	859	289	1049	1007	181	148	312	743	894	31	687	873	251	559	671	217	866	359	882	1215	1113	851	1371	226	600	465	1346	423						
San Sebastián/Donostia (E)	1345	450	1186	1345	559	1158	1327	244	870	1128	1132	1119	897	596	1321	1003	1013	1496	895	673	1192	462	1192	877	746	1222	570	904	1139	699	822	545	958	1289					
St-Malo (F)	858	943	699	858	1143	960	840	517	220	637	645	517	195	624	834	688	912	1009	268	221	705	496	786	840	1090	1277	178	1245	614	416	963	552	802	757					
Strasbourg (F)	607	1126	475	520	1135	242	332	1061	1076	546	432	621	843	661	608	341	397	683	691	683	388	748	223	508	824	496	863	844	557	612	488	955	346	576	1301	895			
Toulouse (F)	1222	188	1063	1222	389	821	1204	245	871	1005	1009	996	898	383	1198	751	676	1373	848	674	1069	307	1085	540	409	885	571	567	1016	575	699	208	835	1166	345	758	1047		
Tours (F)	760	775	601	760	975	691	742	349	500	543	547	534	373	308	736	418	642	910	310	88	607	221	607	472	774	920	215	929	554	114	237	795	373	704	589	319	716	590	
Vlissingen (NL)	207	1230	88	216	1513	820	309	928	882	49	135	162	618	772	148	674	860	358	434	550	204	744	346	869	1202	1074	730	1358	76	479	343	1333	327	110	1168	677	563	1145	583

→

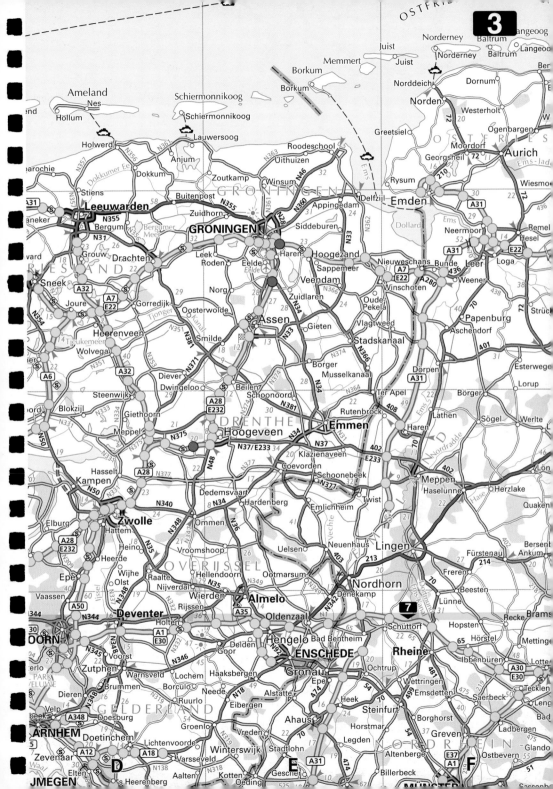

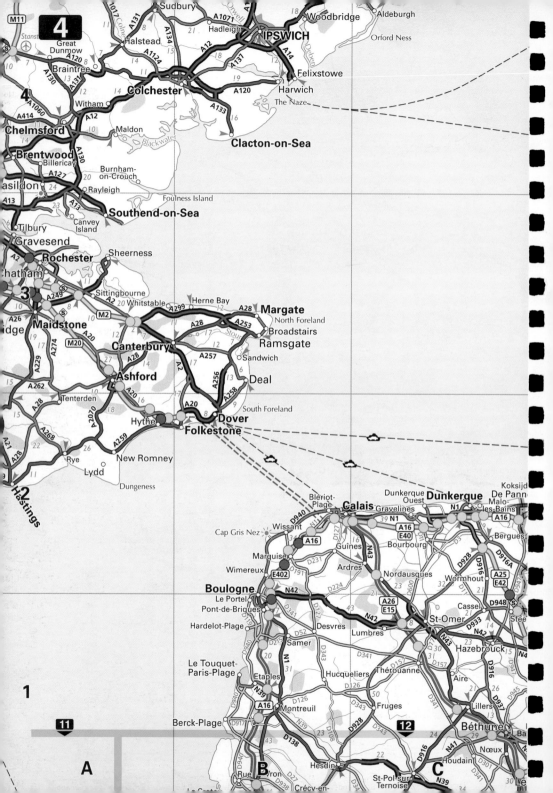

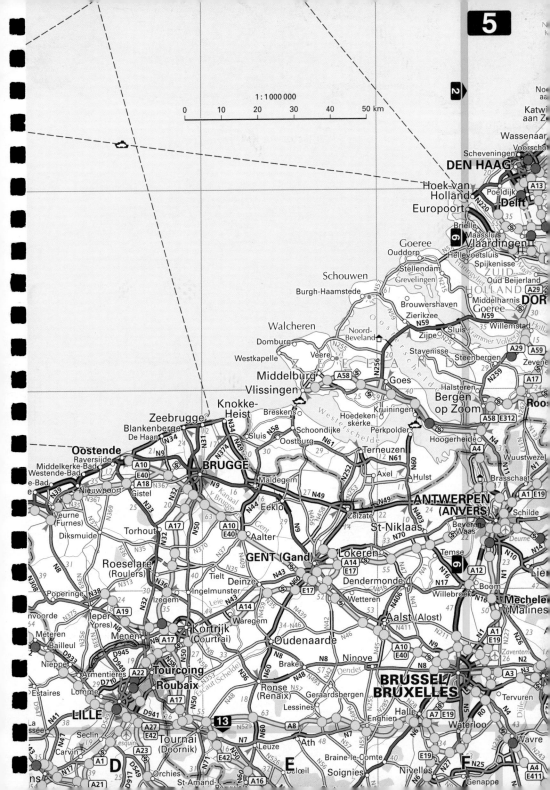

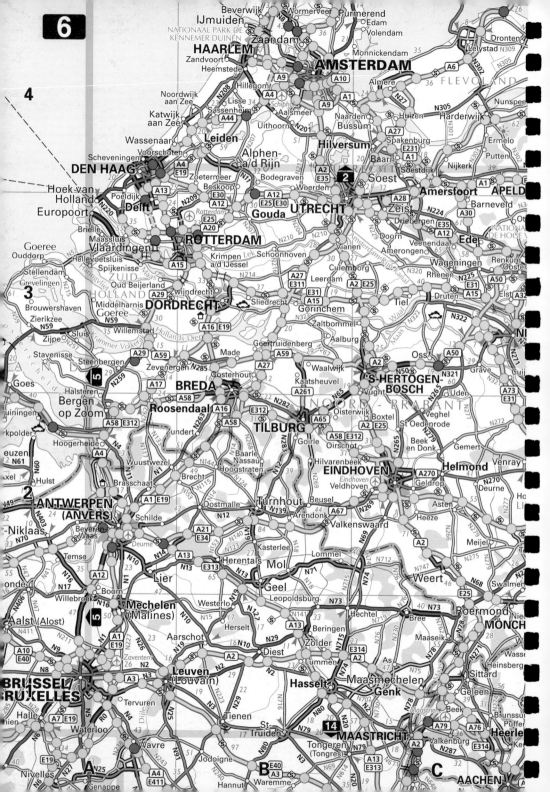

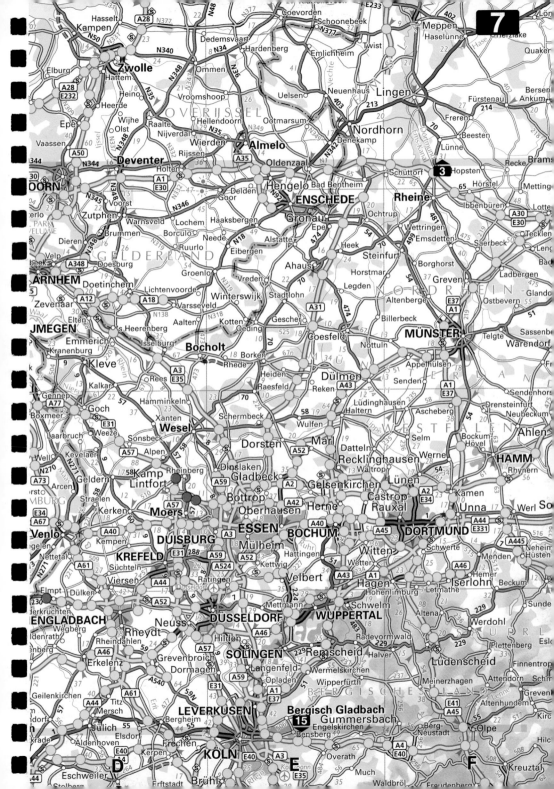

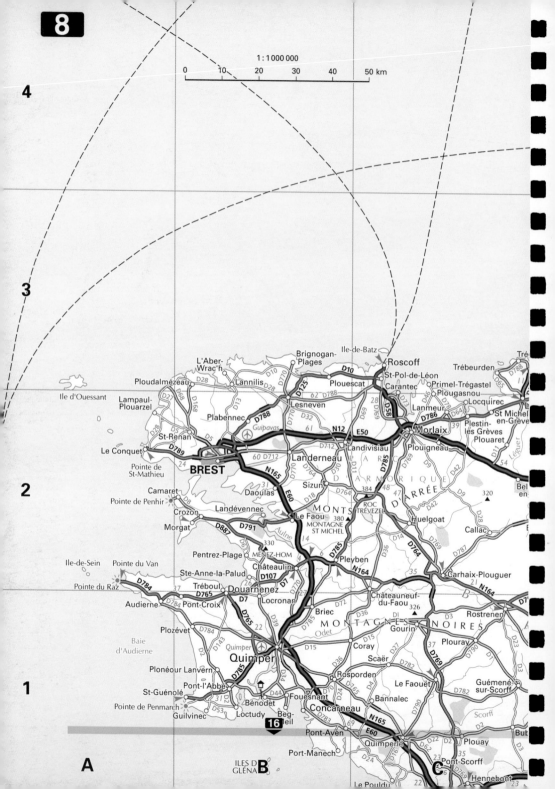

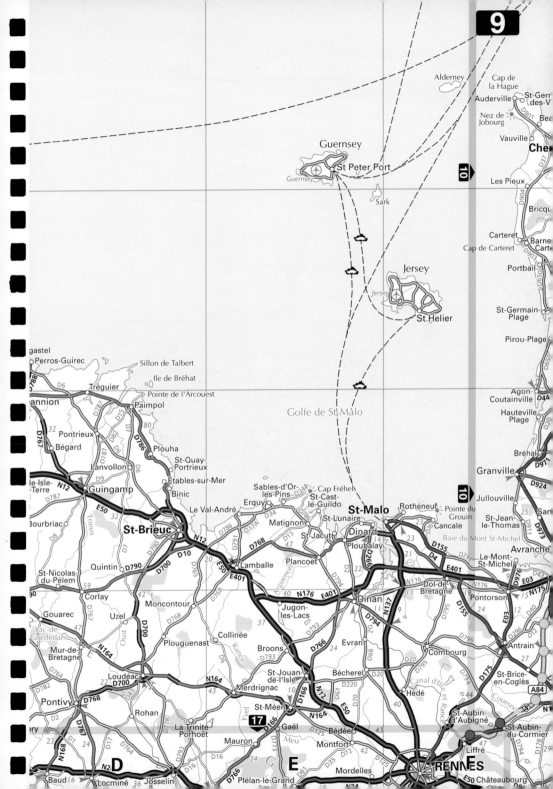

9

Alderney

Cap de
la Hague

Auderville   St-Gerr
des-V

Nez de   Bea
Jobourg

Vauville

Che

Guernsey

St Peter Port   **10**

Guernsey   Les Pieux

Sark   Bricqu

Carteret   Barne
Cap de Carteret   Cart

Jersey   Portbail

Jersey   St-Germain-
Plage

St Helier   Pirou-Plage

Golfe de St-Malo   Agon-
Coutainville   D44

gastel   Hauteville
Perros-Guirec   Plage
Sillon de Talbert

Ile de Bréhat   Bréhal
D6   Tréguier

annion   Pointe de l'Arcouest   Granville   D924
Paimpol
D787   Pontrieux   D786   Plouha   Jullouville   **10**
Bégard   St-Quay-
Portrieux   Bréhal
Lanvollon   Étables-sur-Mer   Granville   D911
le-Isle-   Guingamp   Binic   Sables-d'Or-   Cap Fréhel   Rothéneuf   Pointe du   St-Jean-
Terre   N12   les-Pins   St-Cast-   Grouin   le-Thomas   Sari
D787   E50   Erquy   lé-Guildo   **St-Malo**   Cancale
Bourbriac   Le Val-André   St-Lunaire   Baie du Mont St-Michel
Trieux   D34   Matignon   St-Jacut   Dinard   23   D155   Le-Mont-   Avranche
St-Brieuc   D786   Ploubalay   St-Michel
Quintin   D790   N12   D791   D768   Plancoët   Dol-de-   E401   D976   E03
St-Nicolas-   D700   Lamballe   E50   Bretagne   N176   Pontorson   N175
du-Pélem   D765   E401   Jugon-   N176   D155
Corlay   D768   les-Lacs   Dinan   Dol-de-   Antrain
Gouarec   Uzel   Moncontour   D794   Bretagne   Pontorson   D40
D767   Plouguenast   Collinée   D793   Evran   D20   Combourg   St-Brice-
Mur-de-   N164   Broons   D766   Bécherel   D795   D175   en-Coglès
Bretagne   D793   D98   D20   A84
D764   Loudéac   N164   St-Jouan-   D166   Hédé   Canal d'Ille   St-Aubin-
Pontivy   D768   D700   Merdrignac   de-l'Isle   N12   D61   et Rance   d'Aubigné   N
D2   Rohan   St-Méen   N164   St-Aubin-
D767   La Trinité-   **17**   Gaël   D125   Bédée   du-Cormier
N168   Porhoët   Mauron   Meu   Montfort   Liffré
D2   N2   D   Plélan-le-Grand   E   Mordelles   **RENNES**
Baud   Locminé   Josselin   D766   Montfort-sur-Meu   Châteaubourg

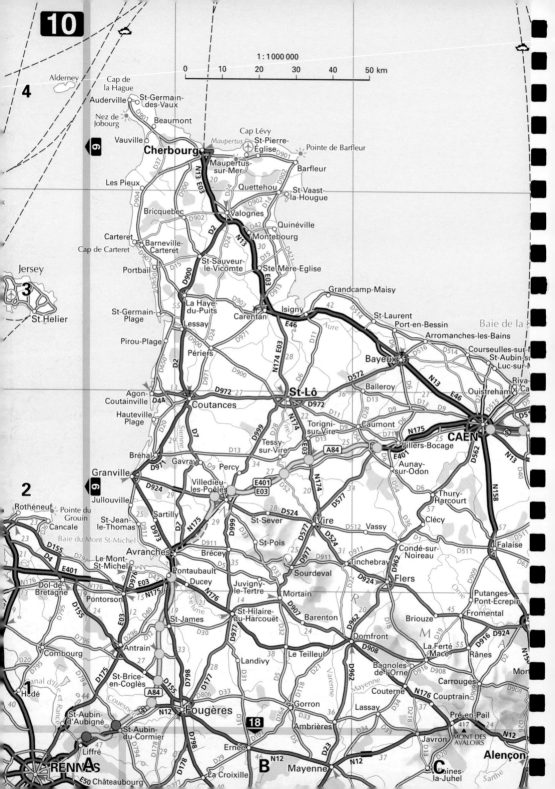

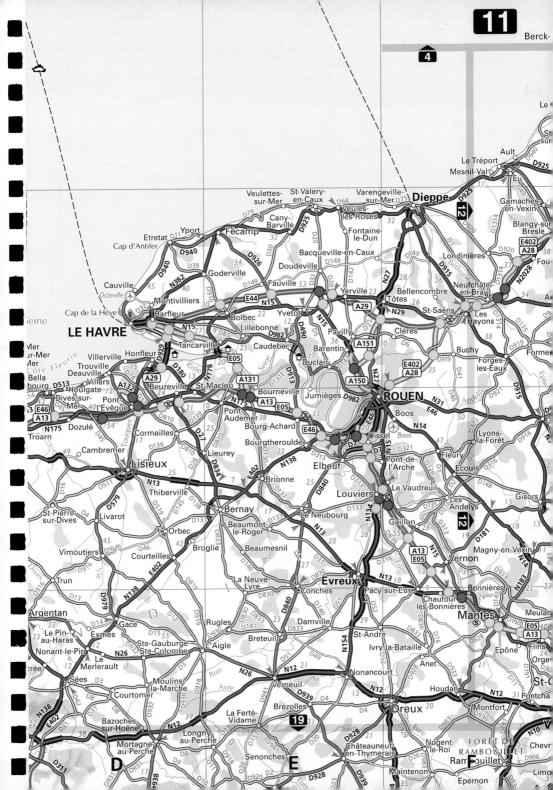

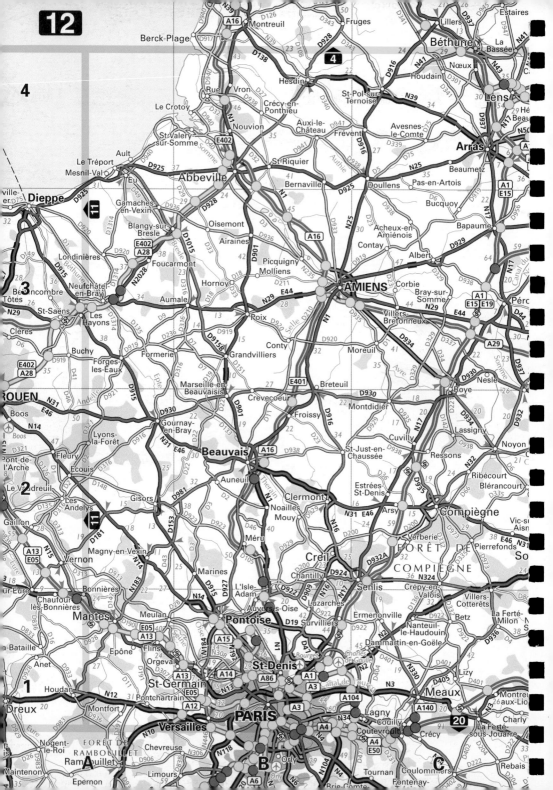

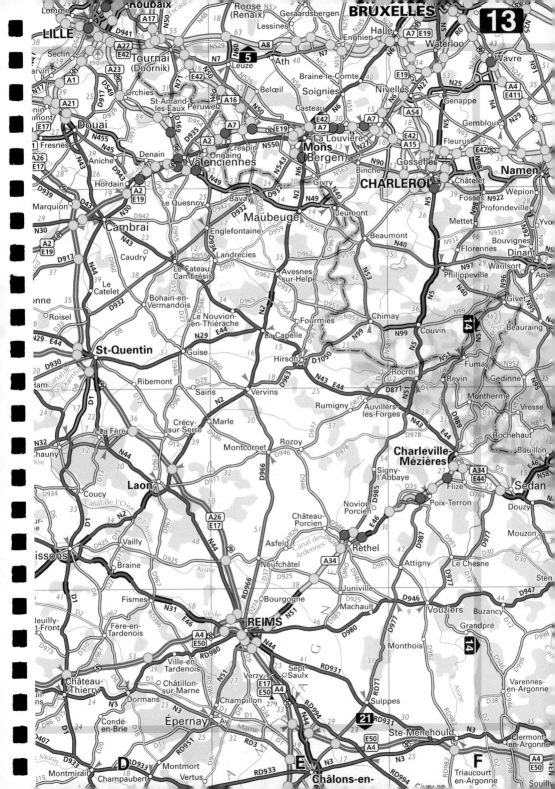

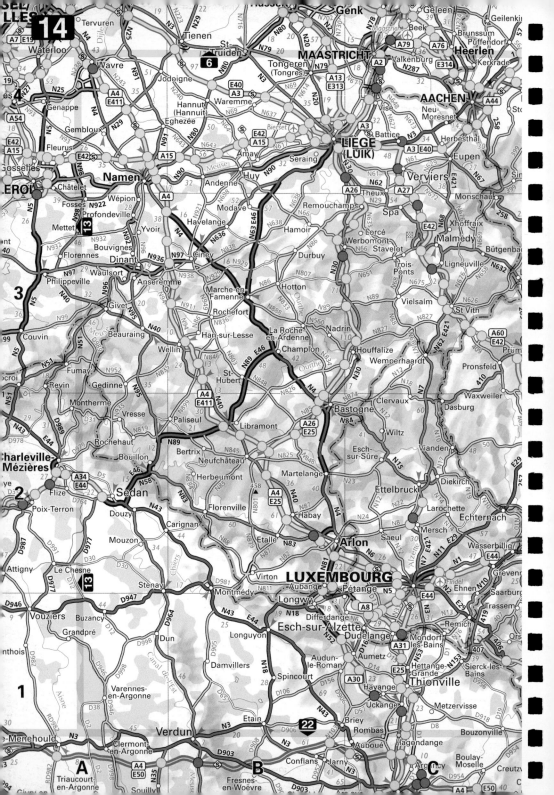

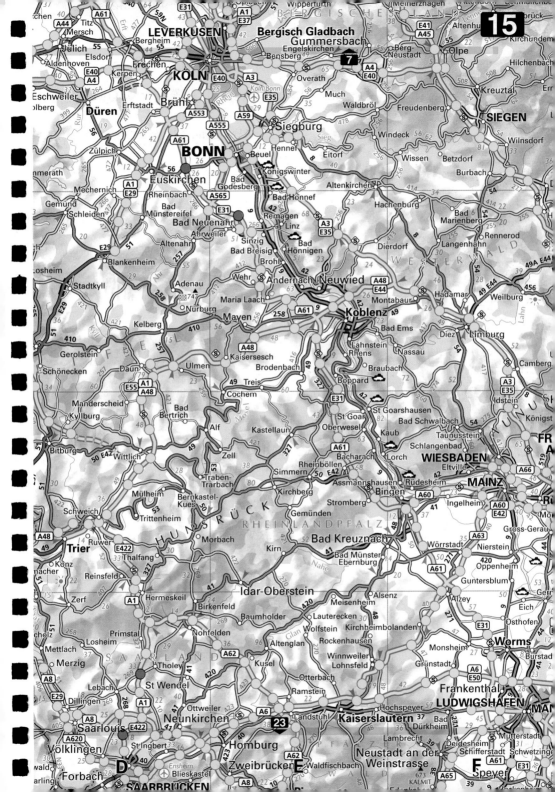

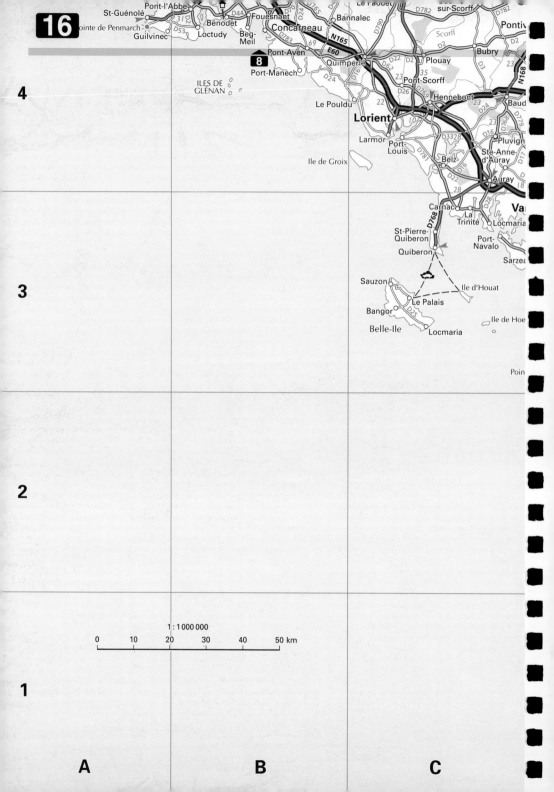

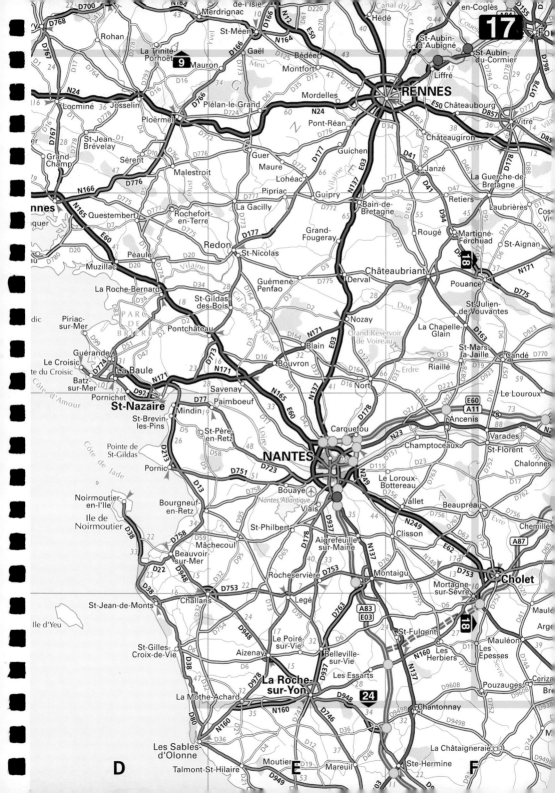

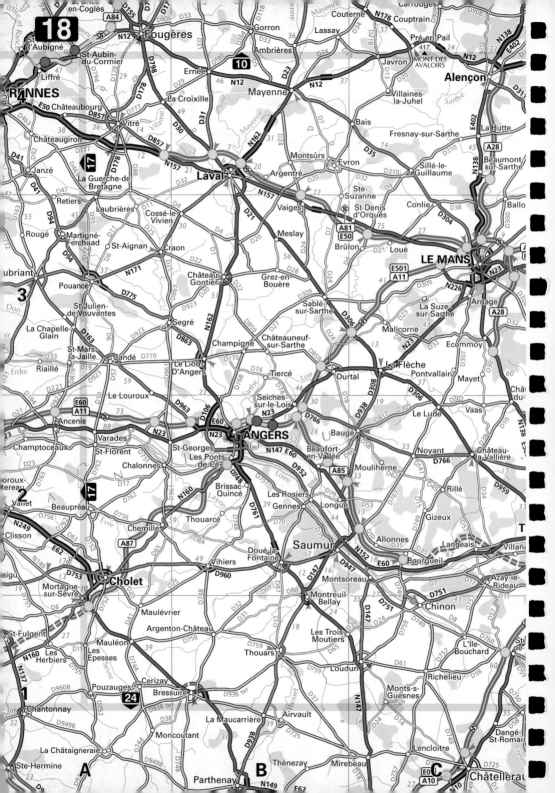

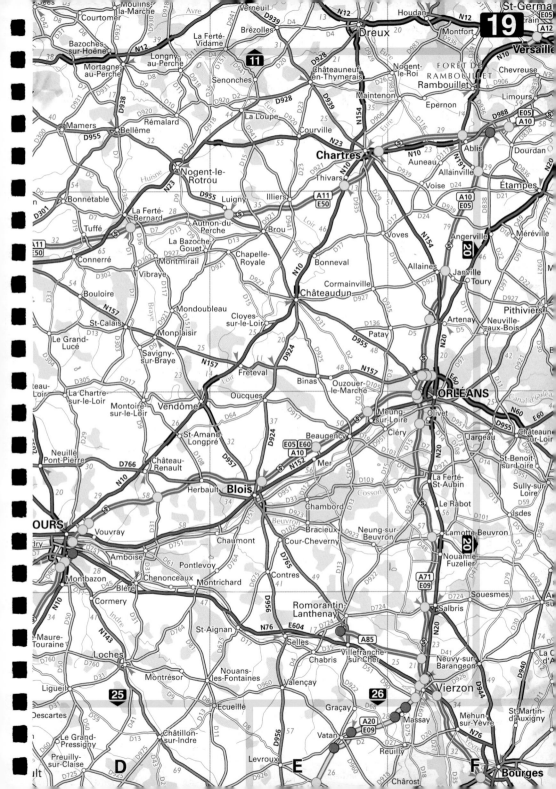

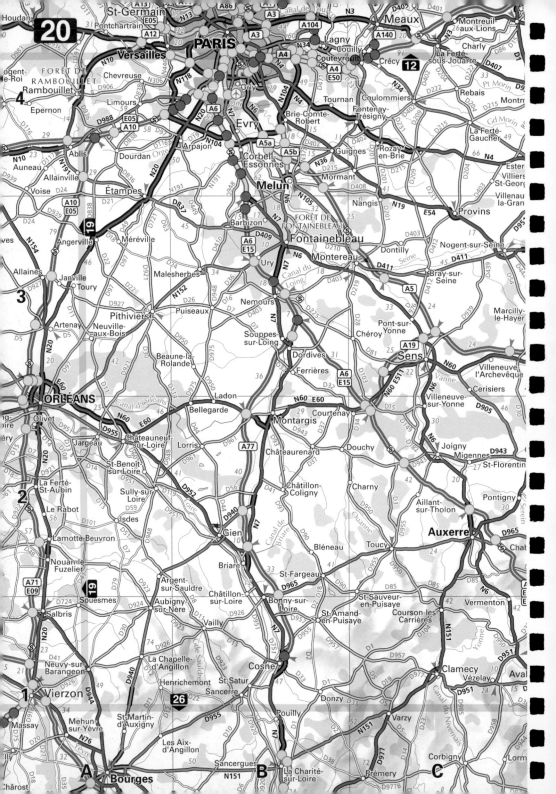

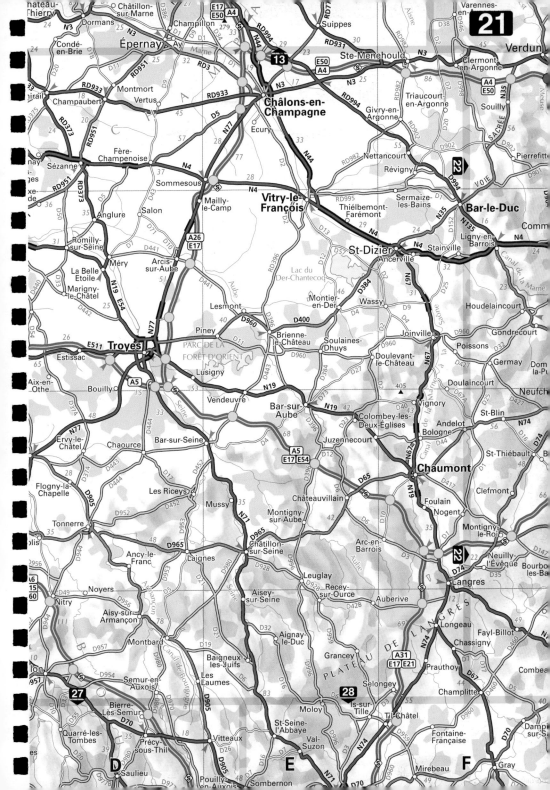

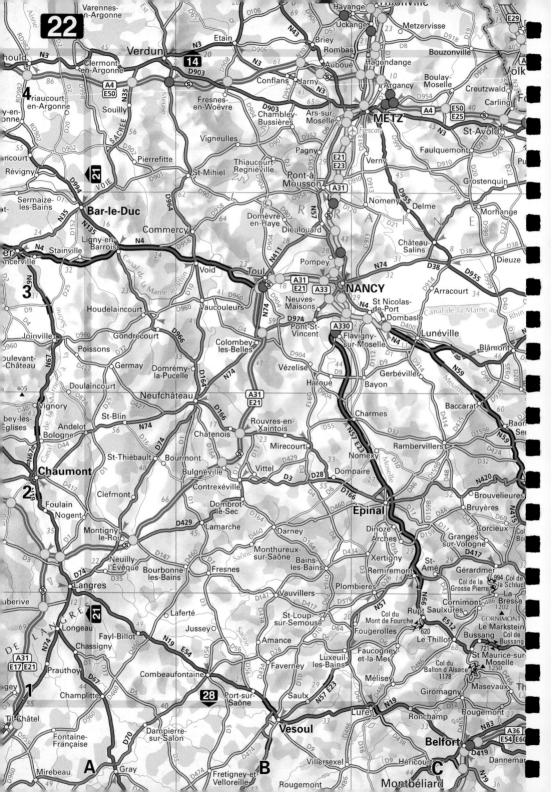

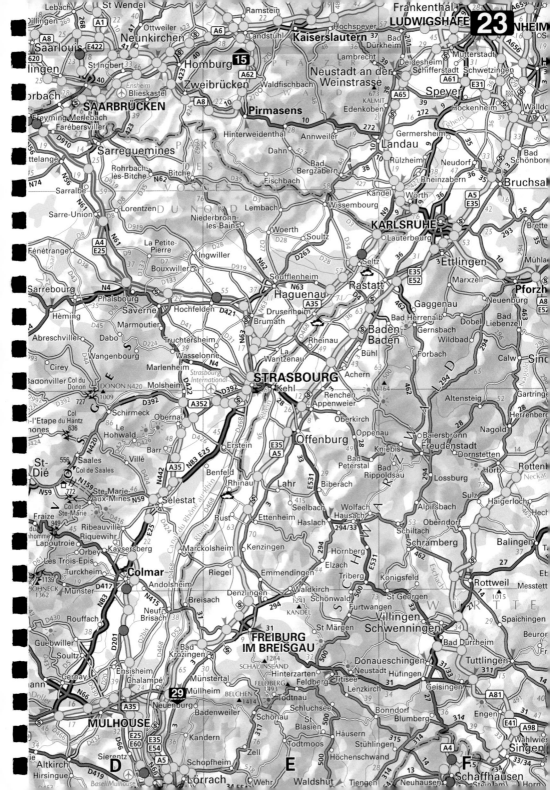

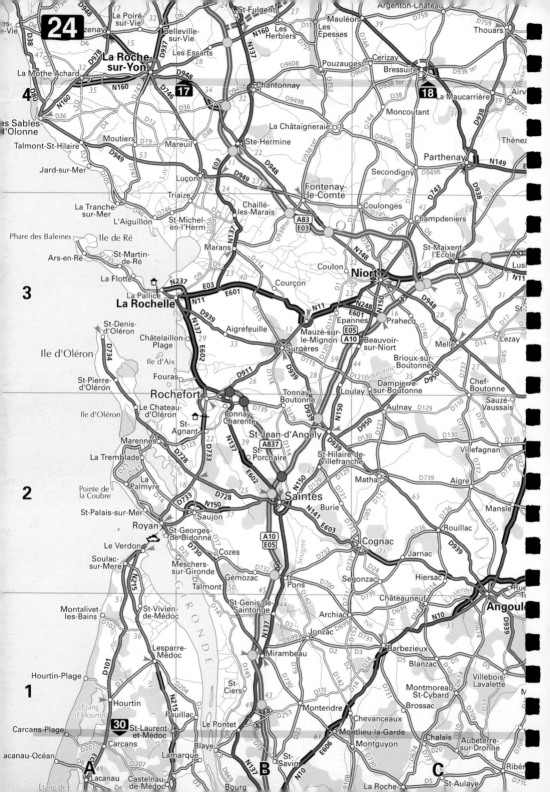

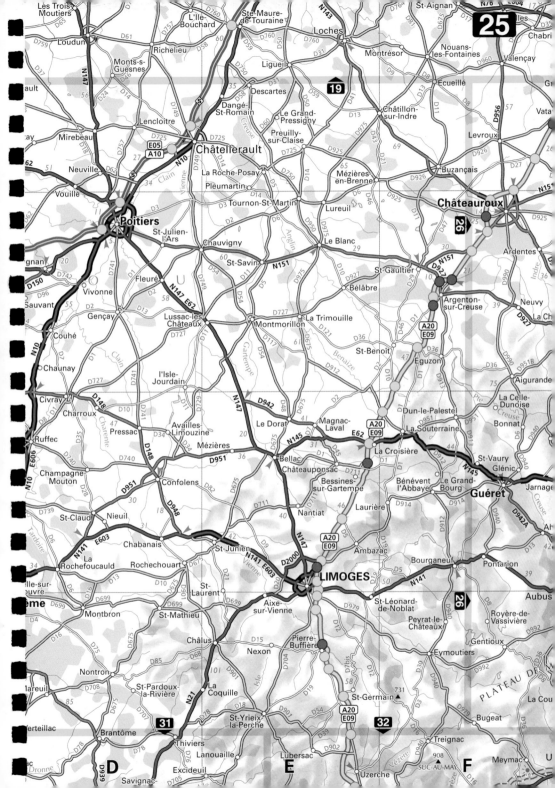

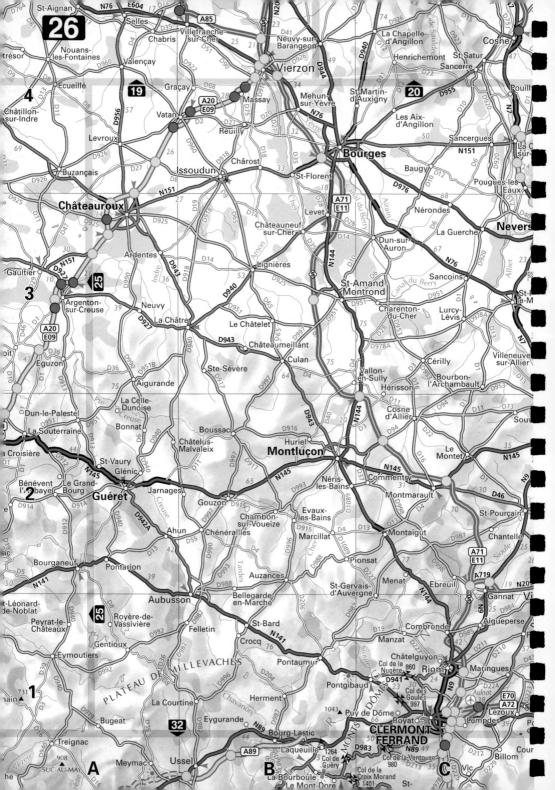

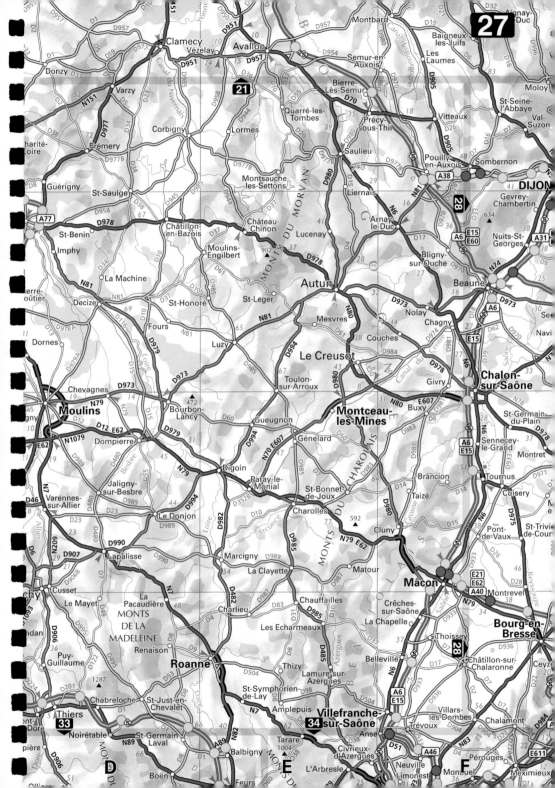

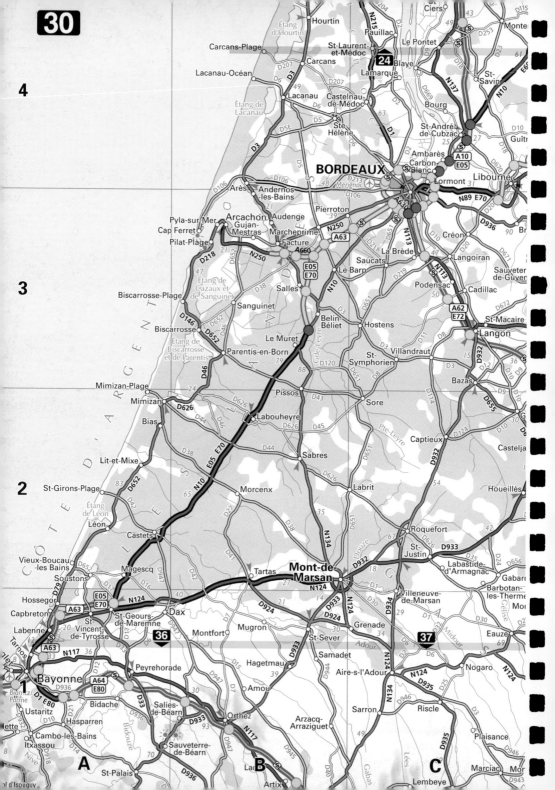

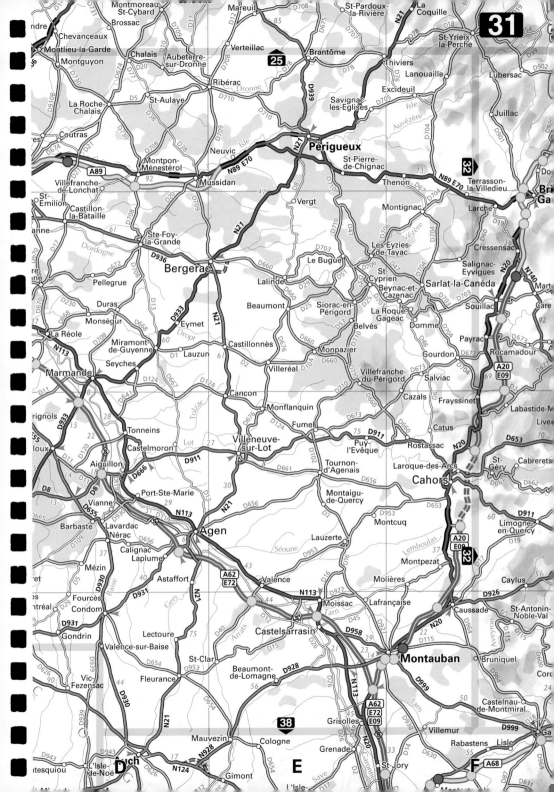

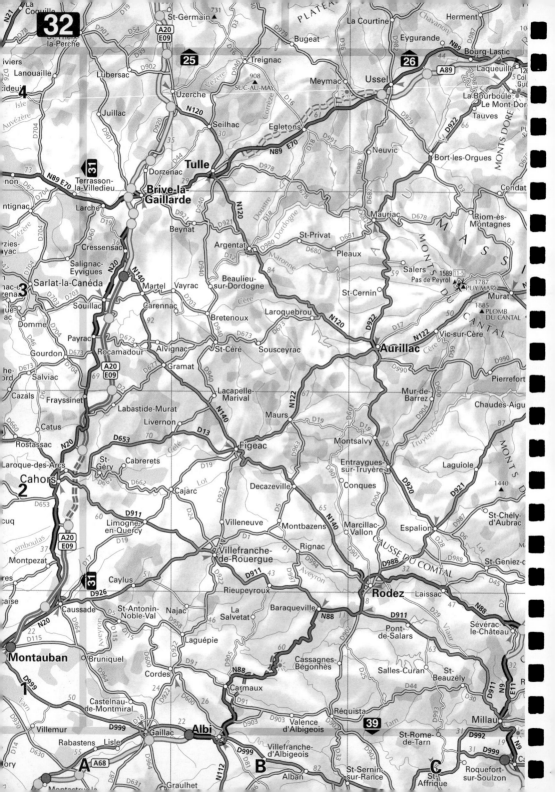

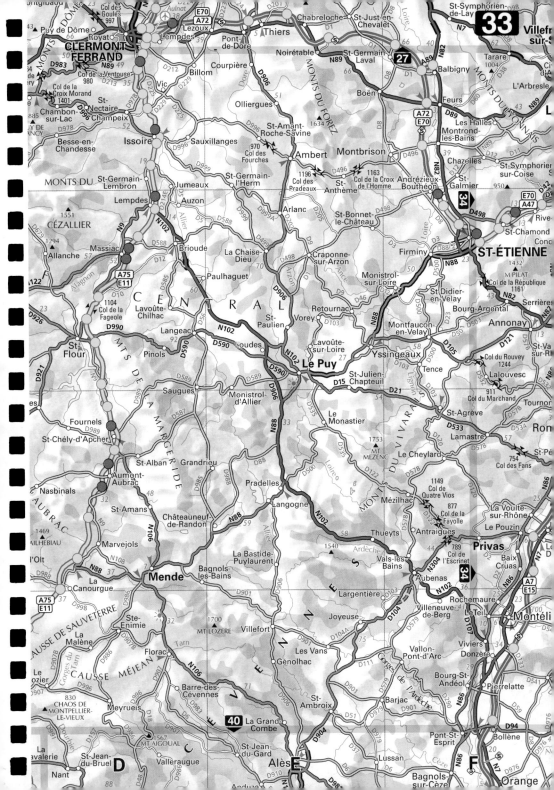

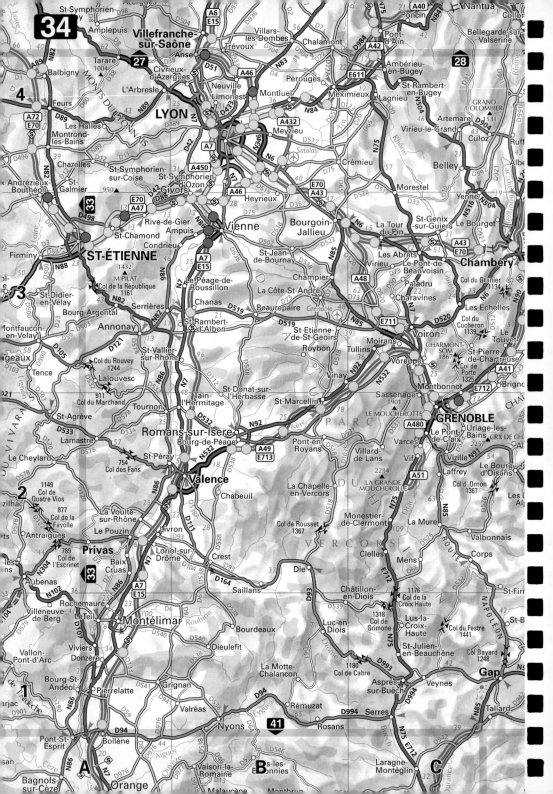

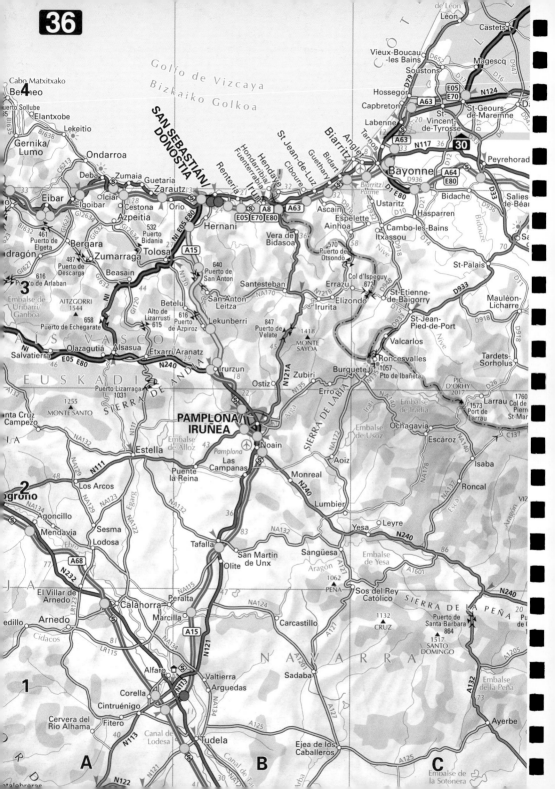

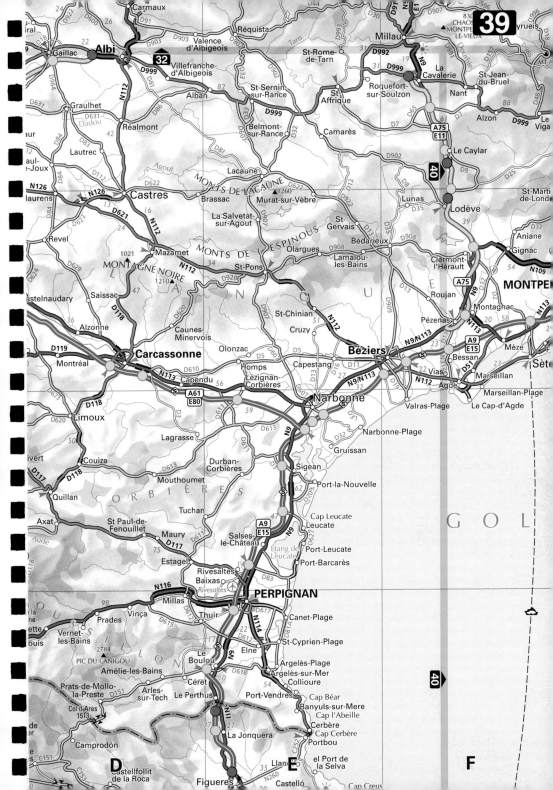

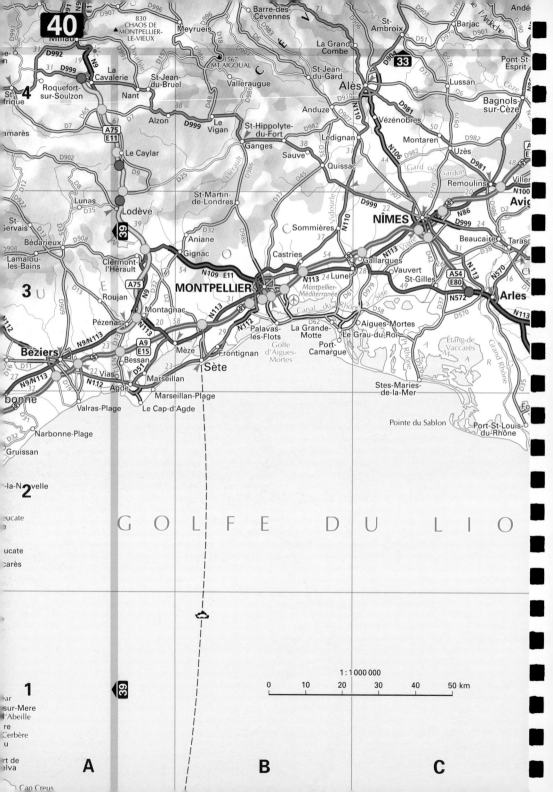

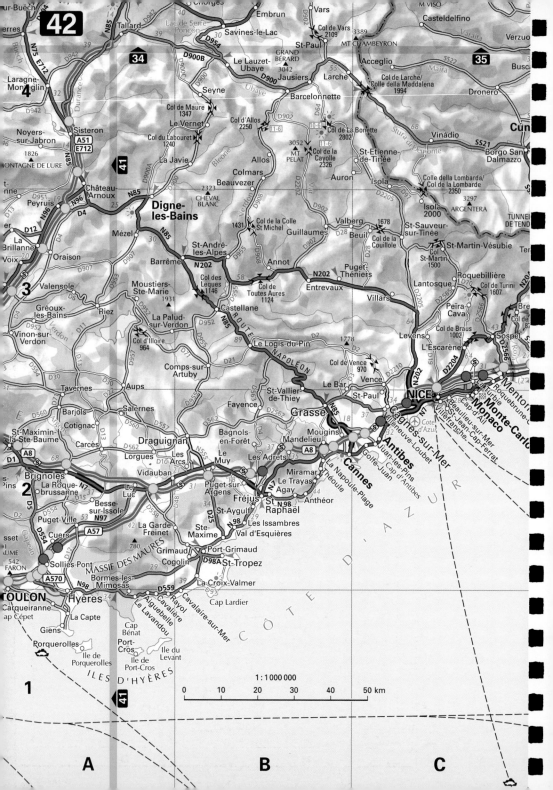

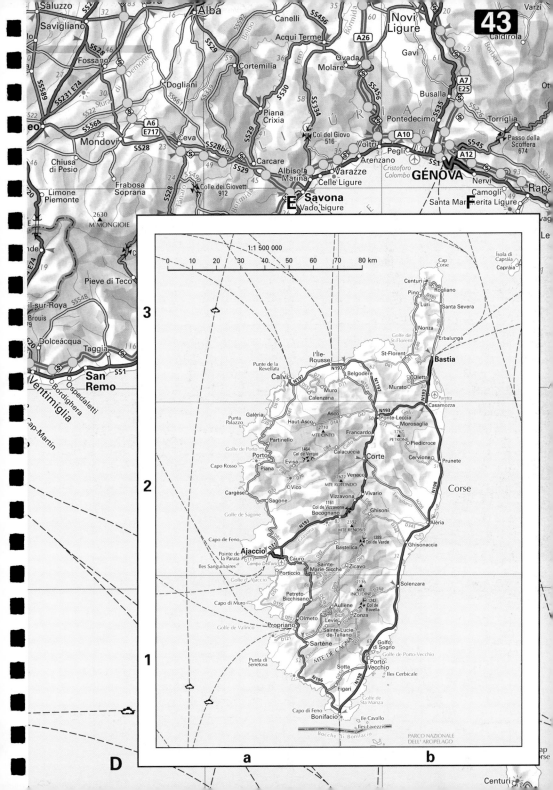

A

Aachen D 14 C4
Aalburg NL 6 B3
Aalsmeer NL 2 B2
Aalst (Alost) B 5 F1
Aalten NL 7 D3
Aalter B 5 E2
Aarau CH 29 F3
Aarberg CH 29 E3
Aarburg CH 29 F3
Aarschot B 6 B1
Abbeville F 12 B4
Ablis F............................ 19 F4
Abondance F 29 D1
Abreschviller F 23 D3
Abriès F 35 E1
Acceglio I 42 C4
Accous F 37 D2
Achern D 23 E3
Acheux-
   en-Amiénois F 12 C3
Acqui Terme I 43 E4
Adelboden CH 29 E1
Adenau D 15 D3
Agay F............................ 42 B2
Agde F............................ 40 A3
Agen F............................ 31 D2
Agon-Coutainville F 10 A2
Agoncillo E 36 A2
Ahaus D 7 E3

Ahlen D 7 F2
Ahrweiler D 15 E3
Ahun F............................ 26 A2
Aigle CH........................ 29 D1
Aignay-le-Duc F 21 E1
Aigre F............................ 24 C2
Aigrefeuille F 24 B3
Aigrefeuille-
   sur-Maine F 17 E2
Aiguebelle F 42 A1
Aiguebelle F 35 D3
Aigueperse F 26 C1
Aigues-Mortes F 40 C3
Aiguilles F 35 E1
Aiguillon F 31 D2
Aigurande F 26 A3
Ailefroide F.................... 35 D2
Aillant-sur-Tholon F 20 C2
Aime F............................ 35 E3
Ainhoa F........................ 36 B3
Ainsa E 37 E1
Airaines F 12 B3
Aire F 4 C1
Aire-sur-l'Adour F 37 E4
Airvault F 24 C4
Aisey-sur-Seine F 21 E1
Aissey F 29 D3
Aisy-sur-Armançon F .. 21 D1
Aix-en-Othe F 21 D3
Aix-en-Provence F 41 E2
Aix-les-Bains F.............. 34 C3
Aixe-sur-Vienne F 25 E1
Aizenay F........................ 17 E1
Ajaccio F........................ 43 a2

Ala di Stura I 35 F2
Alba I.............................. 43 D4
Alban F............................ 39 E4
Albens F.......................... 35 D4
Albert F.......................... 12 C3
Albertville F 35 D3
Albi F.............................. 39 D4
Albisola Marina I 43 E4
Aldeburgh GB 4 C4
Aldenhoven D 15 D4
Alençon F 18 C4
Aléria F.......................... 43 b2
Alès F 40 C4
Alf D 15 D2
Alfaro E 36 A1
Alkmaar NL 2 B2
Allaines F 19 F3
Allainville F 19 F4
Allanche F 33 D3
Allemont F 34 C2
Allevard F 35 D3
Allonnes F 18 C2
Allos F............................ 42 B4
Almelo NL...................... 3 E1
Almere NL 2 C2
Alost (Aalst) B.............. 5 F1
Alp E 38 C1
Alpen D 7 D2
Alphen-aan
   den Rijn NL 2 B1
Alpirsbach D 23 F2
Alsasua E 36 A3
Alsenz D 15 E1
Alstätte D 7 E3

Altena D.......................... 7 F1
Altenahr D 15 D3
Altenberge D 7 F3
Altenglan D.................... 15 E1
Altenhundem D 15 F4
Altenkirchen D 15 E4
Altensteig D 23 F2
Altkirch F...................... 29 E4
Altnagelaar F 32 A3
Alvignac F 32 A3
Alzey D.......................... 15 F1
Alzon F............................ 40 A4
Alzonne F 39 D3
Amance F 22 B1
Amancey F 28 C3
Amay B............................ 14 B4
Ambarès F...................... 30 C4
Ambazac F 25 E2
Ambérieu-en-Bugey F.. 34 C4
Ambert F........................ 33 E4
Amboise F 19 D2
Ambrières F 10 B1
Amélie-les-Bains F........ 39 D1
Amerongen NL 6 C3
Amersfoort NL 6 C4
Amiens F 12 B3
Amou F 37 D4
Amphion F 29 D1
Amplepuis F 27 E1
Ampuis F 34 B3
Amsterdam NL 2 B2
Ancenis F........................ 17 F2
Ancerville F 21 F3
Ancy-le-Franc F............ 21 D2
Andelot F........................ 21 F2

Andenne B 14 B4
Andernach D 15 E3
Andernos-les-Bains F 30 B3
Andijk NL 2 C3
Andolsheim F 23 D2
Andorra la Vella AND 38 B1
Andrézieux-
  Bouthéon F 33 F3
Anduze F 40 B4
Anet F 11 F1
Angers F 18 B2
Angerville F 20 A3
Anglet F 36 C4
Anglure F 21 D3
Angoulême F 24 C2
Aniane F 40 B3
Aniche F 13 D4
Anjum NL 3 D4
Anna Paulowna NL .. 2 B3
Annecy F 35 D4
Annemasse F 28 C1
Annonay F 34 A3
Annot F 42 B3
Annweiler D 23 E4
Anse F 34 B4
Anseremme B 14 A3
Anthéor F 42 B2
Antibes F 42 C2
Antraigues F 33 F2
Antrain F 10 A1
Antwerpen
  (Anvers) B 6 A2
Anvers
  (Antwerpen) B 6 A2
Aoiz E 36 B2
Aosta I 35 F3
Apeldoorn NL 7 D4
Appelhülsen D 7 F3
Appenweier D 23 E2
Appingedam NL 3 E3
Apt F 41 E3
Aramits F 37 D3
Aranatz/Etxarri E 36 A3
Arbois F 28 C3
Arc-en-Barrois F 21 F2
Arcachon F 30 B3
Arcen NL 7 D2
Arches F 22 C2
Archiac F 24 B1
Arcis-sur-Aube F 21 D3
Ardentes F 26 A3
Ardres F 4 C2
Arendonk B 6 B2
Arenzano I 43 E4
Arès F 30 B4
Argancy F 22 C4
Argelès-Gazost F 37 E2
Argelès-Plage F 39 E1
Argelès-sur-Mer F 39 E1
Argent-sur-Sauldre F .. 20 A2
Argentan F 10 C1
Argentat F 32 B3
Argentière F 35 E4
Argenton-Château F .. 18 B1
Argenton-
  sur-Creuse F 25 F3
Argentré F 18 B4
Arguedas E 36 B1
Arguis F 37 D1
Arinthod F 28 B2
Arlanc F 33 E3
Arles F 40 C3
Arles-sur-Tech F 39 D1
Arlon B 14 B2
Armentières F 5 D1
Arnage F 18 C3
Arnay-le-Duc F 27 F3
Arnedo E 36 A1
Arnhem NL 7 D3
Arolla CH 35 F4
Arpajon F 20 B4
Arracourt F 22 C3
Arras F 12 C4
Arreau F 37 D2
Arrens-Marsous F 37 D2
Arromanches-
  les-Bains F 10 C3

Ars-en-Ré F 24 A3
Ars-sur-Moselle F 22 B4
Arsy F 12 C2
Artemare F 34 C4
Artenay F 19 F3
Arties E 38 A2
Artix F 37 D3
Arudy F 37 D2
Arvieux F 35 E1
Arzacq-Arraziguet F .. 37 D3
As B 6 C1
Ascain F 36 B3
Ascheberg D 7 F2
Aschendorf D 3 F3
Asco F 43 b2
Asfeld F 13 E2
Ashford GB 4 A3
Aspet F 38 A3
Aspres-sur-Buëch F .. 34 C1
Assen NL 3 E3
Assmannshausen D .. 15 F2
Astaffort F 31 D2
Asten NL 6 C2
Ath B 13 E4
Attendorn D 7 F1
Attigny F 13 F2
Aubagne F 41 E2
Aubange B 14 B2
Aubenas F 33 F2
Auberive F 21 E1
Aubeterre-
  sur-Dronne F 31 D4
Aubigny-sur-Nere F .. 20 A1
Auboué F 22 B4
Aubusson F 26 B1
Auch F 38 A4
Audenge F 30 B3
Auderville F 10 A4
Audeux F 28 C3
Audierne F 8 A1
Audincourt F 29 D4
Audressein F 38 B2
Audun-le-Roman F ... 14 B1
Aullène F 43 a1
Aulnay F 24 C2
Aulus-les-Bains F 38 B2
Ault F 12 A4
Aumale F 12 B3
Aumetz F 14 C1
Aumont-Aubrac F 33 D2
Aunay-sur-Odon F ... 10 C2
Auneau F 19 F4
Auneuil F 12 B2
Aups F 42 A3
Auray F 16 C4
Aurich D 3 F4
Aurignac F 38 B3
Aurillac F 32 C3
Auron F 42 C4
Auterive F 38 C3
Authon-du-Perche F .. 19 D3
Autun F 27 E3
Auvers-s-Oise F 12 B1
Auvillers-les-Forges F . 13 E2
Auxerre F 20 C2
Auxi-le-Château F 12 B4
Auxonne F 28 B3
Auzances F 26 B2
Auzon F 33 D3
Availles-Limouzine F . 25 D2
Avallon F 21 D1
Avenches CH 29 D2
Avesnes-le-Comte F .. 12 C4
Avesnes-sur-Helpe F . 13 E3
Avignon F 41 D3
Avioraz F 29 D1
Avranches F 10 A2
Ax-les-Thermes F 38 C2
Axat F 39 D2
Axel NL 5 E2
Ay F 13 E1
Ayerbe E 36 C1
Azay-le-Rideau F 18 C2
Azpeitia E 36 A3

B

Baarle Nassau NL 6 B2
Baarn NL 2 C1
Baccarat F 22 C2
Bacharach D 15 E2
Bacqueville-
  en-Caux F 11 E3
Bad Bentheim D 7 E4
Bad Bergzabern D 23 E4
Bad Bertrich D 15 D2
Bad Breisig D 15 E3
Bad Dürkheim D 15 F1
Bad Dürrheim D 23 F1
Bad Ems D 15 E3
Bad Godesberg D 15 E4
Bad Herrenalb D 23 F3
Bad Honnef D 15 E3
Bad Hönningen D 15 E3
Bad Kreuznach D 15 E2
Bad Krozingen D 23 E1
Bad Liebenzell D 23 F3
Bad Marienberg D ... 15 F3
Bad Münster
  Ebernburg D 15 E2
Bad Münstereifel D .. 15 D3
Bad Neuenahr D 15 E3
Bad Peterstal D 23 E2
Bad Rippoldsau D ... 23 F2
Bad Säckingen D 29 F4
Bad Schönborn D 23 F4
Bad Schwalbach D ... 15 F2
Baden-Baden D 23 F3
Badenweiler D 29 F4
Badonviller D 22 C3
Bagà E 38 C1
Bagnères-
  de-Bigorre F 37 E2
Bagnères-
  de-Luchon F 37 F1
Bagnoles-de-l'Orne F . 10 C1
Bagnols-en-Forêt F .. 42 B2
Bagnols-les-Bains F .. 33 D2
Bagnols-sur-Cèze F .. 40 C4
Baiersbronn D 23 F2
Baigneux-les-Juifs F . 21 E1
Bailleul F 5 D1
Bain-de-Bretagne F .. 17 E3
Bains-les-Bains F 22 B2
Bais F 18 C4
Baix F 34 A2
Baixas F 39 E2
Balbigny F 33 F4
Balleroy F 10 C3
Ballon F 18 C3
Balme F 35 E2
Balneario
  de Panticosa E 37 D2
Balsthal CH 29 F3
Baltrum D 3 F4
Bandol F 41 E2
Bangor F 16 C3
Bannalec F 8 C1
Banon F 41 E3
Banyuls-sur-Mer F ... 39 E1
Bapaume F 12 C3
Bar-le-Duc F 21 F3
Bar-sur-Aube F 21 E2
Bar-sur-Seine F 21 E2
Baraqueville F 32 B1
Barbaste F 31 D2
Barbezieux F 24 C1
Barbizon F 20 B3
Barbotan-
  les-Thermes F 30 C2
Barcelonnette F 42 B4
Bardonécchia I 35 E2
Barentin F 11 E3
Barenton F 10 B1
Barfleur F 10 B4
Barjac F 33 E1
Barjols F 41 F2
Barneveld NL 6 C3
Barneville-Carteret F . 10 A3

Barr F 23 D2
Barre-
  des-Cévennes F 33 D1
Barrême F 42 B3
Basel CH 29 F4
Basildon GB 4 A4
Bastelica F 43 a2
Bastia F 43 b3
Bastogne B 14 B2
Battice B 14 C4
Batz-sur-Mer F 17 D3
Baud F 16 C4
Baugé F 18 C2
Baugy F 26 C4
Baume-les-Dames F .. 29 D3
Baumholder D 15 E1
Bavay F 13 E3
Bayeux F 10 C3
Bayon F 22 C3
Bayonne F 36 C4
Bazas F 30 C3
Bazoches-
  sur-Hoëne F 11 D1
Beames-de-Venise F . 41 D4
Beasain E 36 A3
Beaucaire F 40 C3
Beaufort-en-Vallée F . 18 B2
Beaufort-
  sur-Doron F 35 E3
Beaugency F 19 E2
Beaulieu-
  sur-Dordogne F 32 B3
Beaulieu-sur-Mer F .. 42 C2
Beaumesnil F 11 E2
Beaumetz F 12 C4
Beaumont F 31 E3
Beaumont F 10 A4
Beaumont B 13 E3
Beaumont-
  de-Lomagne F 31 E1
Beaumont-le-Roger F . 11 E2
Beaumont-
  sur-Sarthe F 18 C4
Beaune F 28 A3
Beaune-la-Rolande F . 20 B3
Beaupréau F 18 A2
Beauraing B 14 A3
Beaurepaire F 34 B3
Beaurepaire-
  en-Bresse F 28 B2
Beauvais F 12 B2
Beauvezer F 42 B4
Beauvoir-sur-Mer F .. 17 D2
Beauvoir-sur-Niort F . 24 C3
Bécherel F 9 E1
Beckum D 7 F2
Bédarieux F 39 F3
Bédée F 17 E4
Bedous F 37 D2
Beek NL 6 C1
Beek en Donk NL 6 C2
Beesten D 3 F1
Beg-Meil F 8 B1
Bégard F 9 D2
Beilen NL 3 E3
Bélábre F 25 E3
Belcaire F 38 C2
Belfort F 29 D4
Belgodère F 43 b3
Belin-Béliet F 30 B3
Bellac F 25 E2
Belle-Isle-en-Terre F . 8 C2
Bellegarde F 20 B2
Bellegarde-
  en-Marche F 26 B2
Bellegarde-
  sur-Valserine F 28 B1
Bellême F 19 D4
Bellencombre F 11 F3
Belleville F 27 F1
Belleville-sur-Vie F ... 17 E1
Belley F 34 C4
Bellver
  de Cerdanya E 38 C1
Belmont-sur-Rance F . 39 E4
Beloeil B 13 E4
Belvès F 31 E3

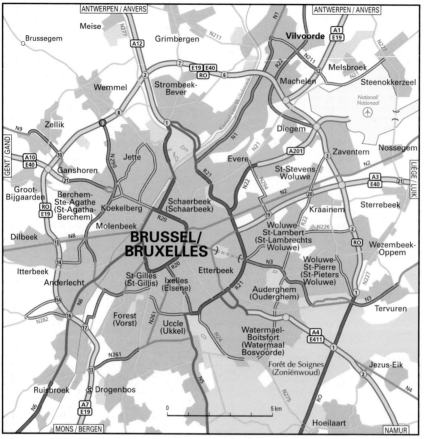

Belz F	16	C4	Betz F	12	C1	Blangy-sur-Bresle F	12	A3
Benasque F	37	E1	Betzdorf D	15	F4	Blankenberge B	5	D2
Bénévent l'Abbaye F	25	F2	Beuel D	15	E4	Blankenheim D	15	D3
Benfeld F	23	E2	Beuil F	42	C3	Blanzac F	24	C1
Bénodet F	8	B1	Beuzeville F	11	D2	Blaye F	30	C4
Bensberg D	15	E4	Beveren-Waas B	5	F2	Bléneau F	20	B2
Berck-Plage F	4	B1	Beverwijk NL	2	B2	Blérancourt F	12	C2
Berg-Neustadt D	7	F1	Bex CH	29	D1	Bléré F	19	D2
Bergara E	36	A3	Beynac-et-Cazenac F	31	F3	Blériot-Plage F	4	B2
Bergen NL	2	B2	Beynat F	32	B3	Bletterans F	28	B2
Bergen (Mons) B	13	E4	Béziers F	39	F3	Blieskastel D	23	D4
Bergen aan Zee NL	2	B2	Biarritz F	36	C4	Bligny-sur-Ouche F	27	F3
Bergen op Zoom NL	6	A2	Bias F	30	A2	Blois F	19	E2
Bergerac F	31	E3	Biberach D	23	E2	Blokzijl NL	3	D2
Bergheim D	7	D1	Bidache F	36	C4	Blumberg D	23	F1
Bergisch Gladbach D	7	E1	Bidart F	36	B4	Bocholt D	7	D3
Bergues F	4	C2	Biel/Bienne CH	29	E3	Bochum D	7	E2
Bergum NL	3	D3	Bielsa E	37	E1	Bockum-Hovel D	7	F2
Beringen B	29	E2	Bienne/Biel CH	29	E3	Bocognano F	43	a2
Bern CH	26	B1	Bierre-Lès-Semur F	27	E4	Bodegraven NL	6	B4
Bernaville F	12	B4	Biescas E	37	D1	Boëge F	28	C1
Bernay F	11	E2	Billerbeck D	7	E3	Boën F	33	E4
Bernkastel-Kues D	15	D2	Billom F	33	D4	Bohain-		
Berre-l'Etang F	41	D2	Binas F	19	E3	en-Vermandois F	13	D3
Bertrix B	14	B2	Binche B	13	E4	Bolbec F	11	E3
Besançon F	28	C3	Bingen D	15	F2	Bollène F	41	D4
Bessan F	40	A3	Binic F	9	D2	Bologne F	21	F2
Besse-			Birkenfeld D	15	D1	Bolsward NL	2	C3
en-Chandesse F	33	D4	Biscarrosse F	30	B3	Boltaña E	37	E1
Besse-sur-Issole F	41	F2	Biscarrosse-Plage F	30	B3	Boltigen CH	29	E2
Bessines-			Bischofsdorp D	15	D2	Bonifacio F	43	a1
sur-Gartempe F	25	E2	Bitche F	23	D4	Bonlieu F	28	C2
Betelu E	36	B3	Blain F	17	E3	Bonn D	15	E4
Béthune F	4	C1	Blâmont F	22	C3	Bonnat F	26	A2

Bonndorf D	23	E1
Bonnétable F	19	D3
Bonneval F	19	E3
Bonneval-sur-Arc F	35	E3
Bonneville F	35	D4
Bonnières F	11	F1
Bonnieux F	41	D3
Bonny-sur-Loire F	20	B1
Boom B	6	A2
Boos F	11	F2
Boppard D	15	E3
Borculo NL	7	D3
Bordeaux F	30	C3
Bordères F	37	E2
Bordighera I	43	D3
Borger NL	3	E3
Börger D	3	F2
Borghorst D	7	F3
Borgo		
San Dalmazzo I	42	C4
Borken D	7	E3
Borkum D	3	E4
Bormes-		
les-Mimosas F	42	A1
Bort-les-Orgues F	32	C4
Boskoop NL	6	B4
Bossost E	37	F1
Bottrop D	7	E2
Bouaye F	17	E2
Boudry CH	29	D2
Bouillon B	14	A2
Bouilly F	21	D3
Boulay-Moselle F	22	C4
Boulogne F	4	B1

Boulogne-
sur-Gesse F 38 A3
Bouloire F 19 D3
Bourbon-
l'Archambault F 26 C3
Bourbon-Lancy F 27 D2
Bourbonne-
les-Bains F 22 B2
Bourbourg F 4 C2
Bourbriac F 9 D2
Bourdeaux F 34 B1
Bourg F 30 C4
Bourg-Achard F 11 E2
Bourg-Argental F 34 A3
Bourg-de-Péage F 34 B2
Bourg-en-Bresse F 28 A1
Bourg-Lastic F 32 C4
Bourg-Madame F 38 C1
Bourg-St-Andéol F 33 F1
Bourg-St-Maurice F 35 E3
Bourganeuf F 25 F2
Bourges F 26 B4
Bourgneuf-en-Retz F 17 D2
Bourgogne F 13 E1
Bourgoin-Jallieu F 34 B3
Bourgtheroulde F 11 E2
Bourgueil F 18 C2
Bourmont F 22 A2
Bourneville F 11 E3
Boussac F 26 B2
Boussens F 38 B3
Bouvignes B 14 A3
Bouvron F 17 E3
Bouxwiller F 23 D3
Bouzonville F 14 C1
Boxmeer NL 6 C2
Boxtel NL 6 C2
Bozel F 35 E3
Bra I 35 F1
Bracieux F 19 E2
Braine F 13 D2
Braine-le-Comte B 13 E4
Braintree GB 4 A4
Brakel B 5 E1
Brancion F 27 F2
Branne F 30 C3
Brantôme F 31 E4
Brassac F 39 D3
Brasschaat B 6 A2
Braubach D 15 E3
Bray-sur-Seine F 20 C3
Bray-sur-Somme F 12 C3
Brécey F 10 B2
Brecht B 6 B2
Breda NL 6 B3
Bree B 6 C1
Bréhal F 10 A2
Breil-sur-Roya F 42 C3
Breisach D 23 D1
Breskens NL 5 E2
Bressuire F 18 B1
Brest F 8 B2
Bretenoux F 32 B3
Breteuil F 12 B3
Breteuil F 11 E1
Breuil-Cervinia I 35 F4
Brézolles F 11 E1
Briançon F 35 D2
Briare F 20 B2
Bricquebec F 10 B3
Brie-Comte-Robert F ... 20 B4
Briec F 8 B1
Brielle NL 6 A3
Brienne-le-Château F ... 21 E3
Brienz CH 29 F2
Briey F 14 B1
Brig CH 29 F1
Brignogan-Plages F 8 B3
Brignoles F 42 B1
Brignoud F 34 C3
Brionne F 11 E2
Brioude F 33 D3
Brioux-
sur-Boutonne F 24 C3
Briouze F 10 C1
Brissac-Quincé F 18 B2
Brive-la-Gaillarde F 32 A3

Broadstairs GB 4 B3
Brodenbach D 15 E3
Broglie F 11 D2
Brohl D 15 E3
Broons F 9 E1
Brossac F 24 C1
Broto E 37 D1
Brou F 19 E3
Brouvelieures F 22 C2
Brouwershaven NL 5 F3
Bruchsal D 23 F4
Brugge B 5 D2
Brühl D 15 D4
Brûlon F 18 C3
Brumath F 23 E3
Brummen NL 7 D3
Bruniquel F 32 A1
Brunssum NL 6 C1
Brussel/Bruxelles B 5 F1
Bruxelles/Brussel B 5 F1
Bruyères F 22 C2
Bubry F 8 C1
Buchy F 11 F3
Bucquoy F 12 C3
Bugeat F 26 A1
Bühl D 23 E3
Buis-les-Baronnies F 41 E4
Buitenpost NL 3 D3
Bulgnéville F 22 B2
Bulle CH 29 D2
Bunde D 3 F3
Burbach D 15 F4
Büren CH 29 E3
Burgdorf CH 29 E3
Burgh-Haamstede NL 5 E3
Burguete E 36 C3
Burie F 24 B2
Burnham-
on-Crouch GB 4 A4
Busalla I 43 F4
Busca I 43 D4
Bussang F 22 C1
Bussum NL 2 C2
Bütgenbach B 14 C3
Buxy F 27 F2
Buzançais F 25 F4
Buzancy F 14 A1

C

Cabourg F 11 D2
Cabrerets F 32 A2
Cadenet F 41 E3
Cadillac F 30 C3
Caen F 10 C2
Cagnes-sur-Mer F 42 C2
Cahors F 31 F2
Cajarc F 32 A2
Calacuccia I 43 a2
Calahorra E 36 A1
Calais F 4 B2
Caldirola I 43 F4
Calenzana F 43 a3
Calignac F 31 D2
Callac F 8 C2
Calvi F 43 a3
Calw D 23 F3
Camarès F 39 E4
Camaret F 8 B2
Camberg D 15 F3
Cambo-les-Bains F 36 C3
Cambrai F 13 D3
Cambremer F 11 D2
Camogli I 43 F3
Campan F 37 E2
Campodón E 39 D1
Cancale F 9 F2
Cancon F 31 E2
Candanchú E 37 D2
Candé F 18 A3
Canelli I 43 E4
Canet-Plage F 39 E1
Canfranc E 37 D2

Cannes F 42 B2
Canterbury GB 4 A3
Canvey Island GB 4 A3
Cany-Barville F 11 E3
Cap Ferret F 30 B3
Cap-d'Ail F 42 C2
Capbreton F 30 A1
Capendu F 39 D3
Capestang F 39 E3
Captieux F 30 C2
Caraman F 38 C3
Carantec F 8 C3
Carbon-Blanc F 30 C4
Carbonne F 38 B3
Carcans F 30 B4
Carcans-Plage F 30 B4
Carcare I 43 E4
Carcassonne F 39 D3
Carcastillo E 36 B1
Carcès F 41 F2
Carennac F 32 B3
Carentan F 10 B3
Cargèse F 43 a2
Carhaix-Plouguer F 8 C2
Carignan F 14 A2
Carignano I 35 F1
Carling F 22 C4
Carmagnola I 35 F1
Carmaux F 32 B1
Carnac F 16 C3
Carpentras F 41 D4
Carquefou F 17 E2
Carqueiranne F 41 E1
Carro F 41 D2
Carrouges F 10 C1
Carry-le-Rouet F 41 D2
Carteret F 10 A3
Carvin F 13 D4
Casamozza F 43 b2
Caselle I 35 F2
Cassagnes-
Bégonhès F 32 B1
Cassel F 4 C1
Cassis F 41 E2
Casteau B 13 E4
Castejón de Sos E 37 E1
Casteldelfino I 35 E1
Castejaloux F 31 D2
Castellamonte I 35 F2
Castellane F 42 B3
Castellfollit
de la Roca E 39 D1
Castelmoron F 31 D2
Castelnau-
de-Médoc F 30 C4
Castelnau-
de-Montmiral F 32 A1
Castelnau-Magnoac F ... 37 F3
Castelnaudary F 38 C3
Castelsarrasin F 31 E1
Castets F 30 A2
Castillon-la-Bataille F ... 31 D3
Castillonnès F 31 E3
Castres F 39 D3
Castricum NL 2 B2
Castries F 40 B3
Castrop-Rauxal D 7 E2
Catus F 31 F2
Caudebec F 11 E3
Caudry F 13 D3
Caumont F 10 C2
Caunes-Minervois F 39 D3
Cauro F 43 a2
Caussade F 31 F1
Cauterets F 37 E2
Cauville F 11 D3
Cavaillon F 41 D3
Cavalaire-sur-Mer F 42 B1
Cavalière F 42 A1
Cavour I 35 F1
Caylus F 32 A2
Cazals F 31 F3
Cazères F 38 B3
Celle Ligure I 43 E4
Centuri F 43 b3
Cerbère F 39 E1
Ceresole Reale I 35 F3

Céret F 39 D1
Cérilly F 26 C3
Cerisiers F 20 C3
Cerizay F 18 A1
Cernay F 23 D1
Cervera
del Río Alhama E 36 A1
Cervione F 43 b2
Cesana Torinese I 35 E2
Cestona E 36 A3
Ceva I 43 D4
Ceyzériat F 28 B1
Chabanais F 25 D2
Chabeuil F 34 B2
Chablis F 21 D2
Chabreloche F 27 D1
Chabris F 19 E1
Chagny F 27 F3
Chaillé-les-Marais F 24 B3
Chalabre F 38 C2
Chalais F 31 D3
Chalamont F 28 A1
Chalampé F 23 D1
Challans F 17 D3
Challes-les-Eaux F 35 D3
Chalon-sur-Saône F 28 A3
Chalonnes F 18 A2
Châlons-
en-Champagne F 21 E4
Châlus F 25 E1
Chambéry F 34 C3
Chambley-
Bussières F 22 B4
Chambon-sur-Lac F 33 D4
Chambon-
sur-Voueize F 26 B2
Chambord F 19 E2
Chamonix-
Mont-Blanc F 35 E4
Champagne-
Mouton F 25 D2
Champagnole F 28 C2
Champaubert F 21 D4
Champdeniers F 24 C3
Champeix F 33 D4
Champéry CH 29 D1
Champex CH 35 E4
Champier F 34 B3
Champigné F 18 B3
Champillon F 13 E1
Champlitte F 22 A1
Champlon B 14 B3
Champtoceaux F 17 F2
Chanas F 34 B3
Chantelle F 26 C2
Chantemerle F 35 D2
Chantilly F 12 B2
Chantonnay F 24 B4
Chaource F 21 D2
Chapelle-Royale F 19 E3
Charavines F 34 C3
Charenton-
du-Cher F 26 C3
Charleroi B 13 F4
Charleville-
Mézières F 13 F2
Charlieu F 27 E1
Charly F 12 C1
Charmes F 22 C2
Charny F 20 C2
Charolles F 27 E2
Chârost F 26 B4
Charroux F 25 D2
Chartres F 19 E4
Chassigny F 21 F1
Château d'Oex CH 29 E1
Château-Arnoux F 41 F4
Château-Chinon F 27 E3
Château-du-Loir F 18 C2
Château-Gontier F 18 B3
Château-la-Vallière F 18 C2
Château-Porcien F 13 E2
Château-Queyras F 35 E1
Château-Renault F 19 D2
Château-Salins F 22 C3
Château-Thierry F 13 D1
Châteaubourg F 17 F4

47

Châteaubriant F 17 F3
Châteaudun F 19 E3
Châteaugiron F 17 F4
Châteaulin F 8 B2
Châteaumeillant F 26 B3
Châteauneuf F 24 C1
Châteauneuf-
de-Randon F 33 E2
Châteauneuf-
du-Faou F 8 C2
Châteauneuf-
du-Pape F 41 D4
Châteauneuf-
en-Thymerais F 19 E4
Chateauneuf-
sur-Cher F 26 B3
Châteauneuf-
sur-Loire F 20 A2
Châteauneuf-
sur-Sarthe F 18 B3
Châteauponsac F 25 E2
Châteaurenard F 20 B2
Châteauroux F 26 A3
Châteauvillain F 21 E2
Châtel F 29 D1
Châtel-St-Denis CH ... 29 D2
Châtelaillon-Plage F .. 24 B3
Châtelet B 13 F4
Châtelguyon F 26 C1
Châtellerault F 25 D4
Châtelus-Malvaleix F . 26 A2
Châtenois F 22 B2
Chatham GB 4 A3
Châtillon I 35 F3
Châtillon-Coligny F 20 B2
Châtillon-en-Bazois F . 27 D3
Châtillon-en-Diois F ... 34 B1
Châtillon-
sur-Chalaronne F 27 F1
Châtillon-sur-Indre F .. 25 E4
Châtillon-sur-Loire F .. 20 B2
Châtillon-
sur-Marne F 13 D1
Châtillon-sur-Seine F . 21 E2
Chaudes-Aigues F 33 D2
Chauffailles F 27 E1
Chaufour-
lès-Bonnières F 11 F1
Chaumergy F 28 B3
Chaumont F 19 E2
Chaumont F 21 F2
Chaunay F 25 D3
Chauny F 13 D2
Chaussin F 28 B3
Chauvigny F 25 D3
Chazelles F 34 A4
Chef-Boutonne F 24 C3
Chelmsford GB 4 A4
Chemillé F 18 A2
Chemin F 28 B3
Chénérailles F 26 B2
Chenonceaux F 19 D2
Cherbourg F 10 B4
Chéroy F 20 C3
Chevagnes F 27 D2
Chevanceaux F 24 B1
Chevreuse F 20 A4
Chieri I 35 F2
Chimay B 13 E3
Chinon F 18 C1
Chiusa di Pesio I 43 D4
Cholet F 18 A2
Chorges F 35 D1
Choye F 28 C4
Ciboure F 36 B3
Cierp-Gaud F 37 F2
Ciney B 14 B3
Cintegabelle F 38 C3
Cintruénigo E 36 A1
Cirey F 23 D3
Ciriè I 35 F2
Civray F 25 D2
Civrieux-
d'Azergues F 34 B4
Clacton-on-Sea GB 4 B4
Clairvaux-les-Lacs F ... 28 B2
Clamecy F 20 C1

Clavières I 35 E2
Clécy F 10 C2
Clefmont F 22 A2
Clelles F 34 C2
Clères F 11 F3
Clermont F 12 B2
Clermont-
en-Argonne F 21 F4
Clermont-Ferrand F ... 26 C1
Clermont-l'Hérault F .. 40 A3
Clerval CH 29 D3
Clervaux L 14 C2
Cléry F 19 E2
Clisson F 17 F2
Cloyes-sur-le-Loir F ... 19 E3
Cluny F 27 F2
Cluses F 35 E4
Cochem D 15 E2
Coesfeld D 7 E3
Coevorden NL 3 E2
Cognac F 24 C2
Cogne I 35 F3
Cogolin F 42 B2
Colchester GB 4 B4
Coligny F 28 B2
Coll de Nargó E 38 B1
Collinée F 9 E1
Collioure F 39 E1
Collonges F 28 B1
Colmar F 23 D2
Colmars F 42 B4
Cologne F 38 B4
Colombey-
les-Belles F 22 B3
Colombey-
les-Deux-Églises F .. 21 E2
Combeaufontaine F ... 22 B1
Combourg F 9 F1
Combronde F 26 C1
Commentry F 26 C2
Commercy F 22 B3
Compiègne F 12 C2
Comps-sur-Artuby F .. 42 B3
Concarneau F 8 B1
Conches F 11 E2
Condat F 32 C3
Condé-en-Brie F 13 D1
Condé-sur-Noireau F . 10 C2
Condom F 31 D1
Condrieu F 34 B3
Conflans F 22 B4
Confolens F 25 D2
Conlie F 18 C3
Connerré F 19 D3
Conques F 32 B2
Contay F 12 C3
Contres F 19 E2
Contrexéville F 22 B2
Conty F 12 B3
Coray F 9 B1
Corbeil-Essonnes F 20 B4
Corbie F 12 C3
Corbigny F 27 D3
Corcieux F 22 C2
Cordes F 32 A1
Corella E 36 A1
Corlay F 9 D1
Cormainville F 19 E3
Cormeilles F 11 D2
Cormery F 19 D1
Cornimont F 22 C1
Corps F 34 C2
Corte F 43 b2
Cortemília I 43 E4
Cosne F 20 B1
Cosne d'Allier F 26 C2
Cossé-le-Vivien F 18 B3
Cossonay CH 29 D2
Cotignac F 41 F2
Couches F 27 F3
Coucy F 13 D2
Couhé F 25 D3
Couilly F 12 C1
Couiza F 39 D2
Coulommiers F 20 C4
Coulon F 24 B3
Coulonges F 24 C3

Couptrain F 10 C1
Cour-Cheverny F 19 E2
Courchevel F 35 E3
Courçon F 24 B3
Courmayeur I 35 E3
Courpière F 33 E4
Courseulles-
sur-Mer F 10 C3
Courson-
les-Carrières F 20 C1
Courteilles F 11 D2
Courtenay F 20 C2
Courtomer F 11 D1
Courtrail
(Kortrijk) B 5 D1
Courville F 19 E4
Coutances F 10 B2
Couterne F 10 C1
Coutevroult F 20 C4
Coutras F 31 D4
Couvet CH 29 D2
Couvin B 13 F3
Cozes F 24 B2
Crans CH 29 E1
Craon F 18 A3
Craponne-
sur-Arzon F 33 E3
Crêches-sur-Saône F .. 27 F1
Crécy F 20 C4
Crécy-en-Ponthieu F . 12 B4
Crécy-sur-Serre F 13 D2
Creil F 12 B2
Crémieu F 34 B4
Créon F 30 C3
Crépy-en-Valois F 12 C2
Crespin F 13 E4
Cressensac F 32 A3
Crest F 34 B2
Creutzwald F 22 C4
Crevecoeur F 12 B2
Crissolo F 35 E1
Crocq F 26 B1
Crozon F 8 B2
Cruas F 34 A2
Cruseilles F 35 D4
Cruzy F 39 E3
Cuers F 41 E2
Cuijk NL 6 C3
Cuiseaux F 28 B2
Cuisery F 28 A2
Culan F 26 B3
Culemborg NL 6 C3
Culoz F 34 C4
Cúneo I 43 D4
Cuorgnè I 35 F2
Cusset F 27 D2
Cuvilly F 12 C2

D

Dabo F 23 D3
Dahn D 23 E4
Dammartin-
en-Goële F 12 C1
Dampierre F 28 C3
Dampierre-
sur-Boutonne F 24 C3
Dampierre-
sur-Salon F 28 C4
Damville F 11 E1
Damvillers F 14 B1
Dangé-St-Romain F ... 25 E4
Dannemarie F 29 E4
Daoulas F 8 B2
Därligen CH 29 F2
Darney F 22 B2
Dasburg D 14 C2
Datteln D 7 E2
Daun D 15 D3
Dax F 30 A1
De Cocksdorp NL 2 C3
De Haan B 5 D2
De Koog NL 2 B3

De Kooy NL 2 B3
De Panne B 5 D2
Deal GB 4 B3
Deauville F 11 D3
Deba E 36 A4
Decazeville F 32 B2
Decize F 27 D3
Dedemsvaart NL 3 D2
Deidesheim D 23 F4
Deinze B 5 E2
Delden NL 7 E4
Delémont CH 29 E4
Delft NL 6 A3
Delfzijl NL 3 E3
Delle F 29 E4
Delme F 22 C3
Den Burg NL 2 B3
Den Haag NL 6 A4
Den Helder NL 2 B3
Den Oever NL 2 C3
Denain F 13 D4
Dendermonde B 5 F2
Denekamp NL 3 E1
Denzlingen D 23 E1
Derval F 17 E3
Descartes F 25 E4
Desvres F 4 B1
Deurne NL 6 C2
Deventer NL 7 D4
Die F 34 B2
Diekirch L 14 C2
Dieppe F 11 F3
Dierdorf D 15 E3
Dieren NL 7 D3
Diest B 6 B1
Dieulefit F 34 B1
Dieulouard F 22 B3
Dieuze F 22 C3
Diever NL 3 D3
Diez D 15 F3
Differdange L 14 C1
Digne-les-Bains F 42 A3
Digoin F 27 E2
Dijon F 28 B4
Diksmuide B 5 D2
Dillingen D 15 D1
Dinan F 9 E1
Dinant B 14 A3
Dinard F 9 E2
Dinozé F 22 C2
Dinslaken D 7 E2
Dives-sur-Mer F 11 D2
Divonne-les-Bains F 28 C1
Dobel D 23 F3
Doesburg NL 7 D3
Doetinchem NL 7 D3
Dogliani I 43 D4
Dokkum NL 3 D4
Dol-de-Bretagne F 9 F2
Dolceácqua I 43 D3
Dole F 28 B3
Dombasle F 22 C3
Dombrot-le-Sec F 22 B2
Domburg NL 5 E3
Domèvre-en-Haye F ... 22 B3
Domfront F 10 B1
Domme F 31 F3
Dompaire F 22 B2
Dompierre F 27 D2
Domrémy-
la-Pucelle F 22 B3
Donaueschingen D 23 F1
Donostia/
San Sebastián E 36 B3
Dontilly F 20 C3
Donzenac F 32 A4
Donzère F 34 A1
Donzy F 20 B1
Doorn NL 6 C3
Doornik (Tournai) B 13 D4
Dordives F 20 B3
Dordrecht NL 6 B3
Dormagen D 7 E1
Dormans F 13 D1
Dornes F 27 D3
Dornstetten D 23 F2
Dornum D 3 F4

FwAA4WAyDAAAAAA=

6wGCwFmAAE=

7qAAYNY=

4qAAE=

/kRQAYCg=

3/kQAAQAhoOA=

mACLwAGggIhY=

0vAACWABQRHw=

7kAUAQAGw4Ag=

4ABKTgCgOC4A=

7GwAQAAEQ8B8=

1JAAEYAhQLAA=

1JAAEYAhQLAA=

5cAAUATH4KAw=

4mAAsAHCQMEQ=

/xQAfCHgyDA=

mwALgAkSBg6A=

2JAAMY8BECgA=

2WAA4QBBAGAw=

4mAAEADI4ag=

5CAA4ABBwIBQ=

0XAAIQBAgIAw=

3GAAUAGiwMEA=

2LAAQQDgwDBw=

+mAAYJgwTA=

7oAAcAHAwGAw=

mXAA0IAwTHw=

9GAAEIAxQDAA=

2LAAoIAwQBAw=

2JAA0IAggCAw=

+JAAsEAYIAw=

2KAAUAGiQMEA=

5OAA0EAYIAw=

3KAAkAHhQFAg=

7oAAcAHAwGAw=

5mAAEADIwag=

2VAA8EAcIAg=

2KAAYABggNAA=

0bAAMAHBQDAQ=

2HAAIIAwTDg=

2VAA8EAYHAw=

3KAAkAHhQFAg=

+JAAkIAYHAg=

3KAAkAHhQFAg=

2XAA4AHhwFAg=

2KAAYABggNAA=

0bAAMAHBQDAQ=

2HAAIIAwTDg=

2VAA8EAYHAw=

3KAAkAHhQFAg=

+JAAkIAYHAg=

3KAAkAHhQFAg=

2XAA4AHhwFAg=

2KAAYABggNAA=

0bAAMAHBQDAQ=

2HAAIIAwTDg=

2VAA8EAYHAw=

3KAAkAHhQFAg=

+JAAkIAYHAg=

3KAAkAHhQFAg=

2XAA4AHhwFAg=

2KAAYABggNAA=

0bAAMAHBQDAQ=

2HAAIIAwTDg=

2VAA8EAYHAw=

3KAAkAHhQFAg=

+JAAkIAYHAg=

3KAAkAHhQFAg=

2XAA4AHhwFAg=

2KAAYABggNAA=

0bAAMAHBQDAQ=

2HAAIIAwTDg=

2VAA8EAYHAw=

3KAAkAHhQFAg=

+JAAkIAYHAg=

3KAAkAHhQFAg=

2XAA4AHhwFAg=

2KAAYABggNAA=

0bAAMAHBQDAQ=

2HAAIIAwTDg=

2VAA8EAYHAw=

2VAA8EAYHAw=

2VAA8EAYHAw=

Gennep NL 7 D2
Gennes F 18 B2
Génolhac F 33 E1
Génova I 43 F4
Gent (Gand) B 5 E2
Gentioux F 26 A1
Georgsheil D 3 F4
Geraardsbergen B 5 E1
Gérardmer F 22 C2
Gerbéviller F 22 C3
Germay F 22 A3
Germersheim D 23 F4
Gernsbach D 23 F3
Gerolstein D 15 D3
Gescher D 7 E3
Gevrey-Chambertin F .. 28 A3
Gex F 28 C1
Ghisonaccia F 43 b2
Ghisoni F 43 b2
Gien F 20 B2
Giens F 41 F1
Gieten NL 3 E3
Giethoorn NL 3 D2
Gignac F 40 B3
Gillingham GB 4 A3
Gimont F 38 B4
Giromagny F 22 C1
Gisors F 12 A2
Gistel B 5 D2
Givet F 14 A3
Givors F 34 B3
Givry B 13 E4
Givry F 27 F3
Givry-en-Argonne F 21 F4
Gizeux F 18 C2
Gladbeck D 7 E2
Glénic F 26 A2
Goch D 7 D2
Goderville F 11 D3
Goes NL 5 F3
Goirle NL 6 B2
Golfe-Juan F 42 C2
Golfo di Sogno F 43 b1
Goncelin F 34 C3
Gondrecourt F 22 A3
Gondrin F 31 D1
Goor NL 7 E4
Goppenstein CH 29 E1
Gordes F 41 D3
Gorinchem NL 6 B3
Gorredijk NL 3 D3
Gorron F 10 B1
Gosselies B 13 F4
Gouarec F 9 D1
Gouda NL 6 B3
Goumois CH 29 D3
Gourdon F 31 F3
Gourin F 8 C1
Gournay-en-Bray F 12 A2
Gouzon F 26 B2
Graçay F 26 B4
Grächen CH 29 F1
Gramat F 32 A3
Grancey F 21 E1
Grand-Champ F 17 D4
Grandcamp-Maisy F 10 B3
Grande-Fougeray F 17 E3
Grandpré F 13 F1
Grandrieu F 33 E2
Grandvilliers F 12 B3
Granges-
  sur-Vologne F 22 C2
Granville F 10 A2
Grasse F 42 B2
Graulhet F 39 D4
Grave NL 6 C3
Gravelines F 4 C2
Gray F 28 B4
Great Dunmow GB 4 A4
Greetsiel D 3 F4
Grenade F 30 C1
Grenade F 38 C4
Grenchen CH 29 E3
Grenoble F 34 C2
Gréoux-les-Bains F 41 E3
Greven D 7 F3
Grevenbroich D 7 D1

Grevenbrück D 7 F1
Grevenmacher L 14 C2
Grez-en-Bouère F 18 B3
Grignan F 34 A1
Grignols F 30 C2
Grimaud F 42 B2
Grindelwald CH 29 F2
Grisolles F 31 E1
Groenlo NL 7 E3
Gronau D 7 E3
Groningen NL 3 E3
Grosshöchstetten CH... 29 E2
Grostenquin F 22 C4
Grouw NL 3 D3
Gruissan F 39 E2
Grünstadt D 15 F1
Gruyères CH 29 D2
Gstaad CH 29 E1
Gsteig CH 29 E1
Guebwiller F 23 D1
Guémené-Penfao F 17 E3
Guémené-
  sur-Scorff F 8 C1
Guer F 17 E4
Guérande F 17 D3
Guéret F 26 A2
Guérigny F 27 D4
Guetaria E 36 A4
Guéthary F 36 B4
Gueugnon F 27 E2
Guichen F 17 E4
Guignes F 20 B4
Guillaumes F 42 B3
Guillestre F 35 D1
Guilvinec F 8 B1
Guînes F 4 C1
Guingamp F 9 D2
Guipry F 17 E3
Guise F 13 D3
Guîtres F 31 D4
Gujan-Mestras F 30 B3
Gummersbach D 7 F1
Gunten CH 29 E2
Guntersblum D 15 F2
Gwatt CH 29 E2
Gy F 28 C4

H

Haaksbergen NL 7 E3
Haarlem NL 2 B2
Habay B 14 B2
Hachenburg D 15 F3
Hadamar D 15 F3
Hadleigh GB 4 B4
Hagen D 7 F2
Hagetmau F 37 D4
Hagondange F 22 C4
Haguenau F 23 E3
Halle B 5 F1
Halstead GB 4 A4
Halsteren NL 6 A2
Haltern D 7 E2
Halver D 7 F1
Ham F 12 C2
Hamm D 7 F2
Hamminkeln D 7 D2
Hamoir B 14 B3
Han-sur-Lesse B 14 B3
Hannuit (Hannut) B..... 14 B4
Hannut (Hannuit) B..... 14 B4
Hardelot-Plage F 4 B1
Hardenberg NL 3 E2
Harderwijk NL 2 C2
Haren NL 3 E3
Haren D 3 F2
Haren NL 3 E3
Harfleur F 11 D3
Harlingen NL 2 C3
Haroué F 22 B3
Harwich GB 4 B4
Haselünne D 3 F2
Haslach D 23 E2

Hasparren F 36 C3
Hasselt B 6 B1
Hasselt NL 3 D2
Hattem D 3 D2
Hattingen D 7 E2
Hausach D 23 E2
Häusern D 23 E1
Haut-Asco F 43 a2
Haute-Nendaz CH 35 F4
Hauteville Plage F 10 A2
Havelange B 14 B3
Hayange F 14 C1
Hazebrouck F 4 C1
Hechtel B 6 B1
Hédé F 9 F1
Heek D 7 E3
Heemstede NL 2 B2
Heerde NL 3 D2
Heerenveen NL 3 D3
Heerlen NL 6 C1
Heeze NL 6 C2
Heiden D 7 E3
Heino NL 3 D2
Heinsberg D 7 D1
Hellendoorn NL 3 D2
Hellevoetsluis NL 6 A3
Helmond F 6 C2
Hemer D 7 F2
Hèming F 23 D3
Hendaye F 36 B3
Hengelo NL 7 E4
Hénin Beaumont F 13 D4
Hennebont F 16 C4
Hennef D 15 E4
Henrichemont F 20 A1
Herbault F 19 D2
Herbesthal B 14 C4
Herbeumont B 14 B2
Herentals B 6 B2
Héricourt F 29 D4
Hérisson F 26 C3
Herment F 26 B1
Hermeskeil D 15 D1
Hernani E 36 B3
Herne D 7 E2
Herne Bay GB 4 B3
Herselt B 6 B1
Herzlake D 3 F2
Hesdin F 12 B4
Hesel D 3 F1
Hettange-Grande F 14 C1
Heyrieux F 34 B3
Hiersac F 24 C2
Hilchenbach D 15 F4
Hilden D 7 E1
Hillegom NL 2 B2
Hilterfingen CH 29 E2
Hilvarenbeek NL 6 B2
Hilversum NL 2 C1
Hinterweidenthal D 23 E4
Hinterzarten D 23 E1
Hirsingue F 29 E4
Hirson F 13 E3
Höchenschwand D 23 E1
Hochfelden F 23 E3
Hochspeyer D 15 E1
Hockenheim D 23 F4
Hoedekenskerke NL 5 F2
Hoek van Holland NL... 6 A3
Hohenlimburg D 7 F2
Hollum NL 3 D4
Holten NL 7 D4
Holwerd NL 3 D4
Homburg D 23 D4
Homps F 39 E3
Hondarribia/
  Fuenterrabia E 36 B4
Honfleur F 11 D3
Hoogerheide NL 6 A2
Hoogeveen NL 3 D2
Hoogezand NL 3 E3
Hoogkarspel NL 2 C2
Hoogstraten B 6 B2
Hoorn NL 2 C2
Hopsten D 7 F4
Horb D 23 F2
Hordain F 13 D4

Hornberg D 23 E2
Hornoy F 12 B3
Horst NL 7 D2
Hörstel D 7 F3
Horstmar D 7 F3
Hossegor F 30 A1
Hostens F 30 C3
Hotton B 14 B3
Houdain F 12 C4
Houdan F 11 F1
Houdelaincourt F 22 A3
Houeillès F 30 C2
Houffalize B 14 C3
Houlgate F 11 D3
Hourtin F 24 A1
Hourtin-Plage F 24 A1
Hucqueliers F 4 B1
Huelgoat F 8 C2
Hüfingen D 23 F1
Huizen NL 2 B2
Huizen NL 2 C2
Hulst NL 5 F2
Huriel F 26 B2
Huttwil CH 29 F3
Huy B 14 B4
Hyères F 41 F1
Hythe GB 4 A2

I

l'Ile-Rousse F 43 a3
Ibbenburen D 7 F3
Iciar E 36 A3
Idar-Oberstein D 15 E2
Idstein D 15 F2
Ieper (Ypres) B 5 D1
IJmuiden NL 2 B2
Illiers F 19 E3
Imphy F 27 D3
Ingelheim D 15 F2
Ingelmunster B 5 D1
Ingwiller F 23 D3
Innertkirchen CH 29 F2
Ins CH 29 E3
Interlaken CH 29 F2
Ipswich GB 4 B4
Irun E 36 B3
Iruñea/Pamplona E...... 36 B2
Irurita E 36 B3
Irurzun E 36 B3
Is-sur-Tille F 28 B4
Isaba E 36 C2
Isdes F 20 A2
Iselle F 29 F1
Iserlohn D 7 F2
Isigny F 10 B3
Isola F 42 C4
Isola 2000 F 42 C3
Isona E 38 A1
Isselburg D 7 D3
Issoire F 33 D4
Issoudun F 26 B4
Istres F 41 D3
Itxassou F 36 C3
Ivry-la-Bataille F 11 F1
Izegem B 5 D1
Izernore F 28 B1

J

Jaca E 37 D1
Jaligny-sur-Besbre F 27 D2
Janville F 19 E3
Janzé F 17 F4
Jard-sur-Mer F 24 A4
Jargeau F 20 A2
Jarnac F 24 C2
Jarnages F 26 B2
Jarny F 22 B4

Jaun CH 29 E2
Jausiers F 42 B4
Javron F 18 C4
Jeumont F 13 E3
Jodoigne B 14 A4
Joigny F 20 C2
Joinville F 21 F3
Jonzac F 24 B1
Josselin F 17 D4
Jougne F 28 C2
Joure NL 3 D3
Joyeuse F 33 E1
Juan-les-Pins F 42 C2
Jugon-les-Lacs F 9 E1
Juillac F 32 A4
Juist D 3 F4
Jülich D 7 D1
Jullouville F 10 A2
Jumeaux F 33 D4
Jumièges F 11 E2
Juniville F 13 E1
Jussey F 22 B1
Juvigny-le-Tertre F 10 B2
Juzennecourt F 21 E2

K

Kaatsheuvel NL 6 B3
Kaisersesch D 15 E3
Kaiserslautern D 15 E1
Kalkar D 7 D3
Kamen D 7 F2
Kamp Lintfort D 7 D2
Kampen NL 3 D2
Kandel D 23 F4
Kandern D 29 F4
Kandersteg CH 29 E1
Karlsruhe D 23 F3
Kastellaun D 15 E2
Kasterlee B 6 B2
Katwijk aan Zee NL 2 B2
Kaub D 15 E2
Kaysersberg F 23 D2
Kehl D 23 E3
Kelberg D 15 D3
Kempen D 7 D2
Kenzingen D 23 E2
Kerken D 7 D2
Kerkrade NL 14 C4
Kerpen D 15 D4
Kerzers CH 29 E2
Kettwig D 7 E2
Kevelaer D 7 D2
Kiental CH 29 E2
Kirchberg D 15 E2
Kirchheimbolanden D ... 15 F1
Kirchundem D 15 F4
Kirn D 15 E2
Klazienaveen NL 3 E2
Kleve D 7 D3
Kniebis D 23 F2
Knokke-Heist B 5 E2
Koblenz D 15 E3
Koksijde-Bad B 5 D2
Köln D 15 D4
Königsfeld D 23 F2
Königswinter D 15 E4
Köniz CH 29 E2
Konz D 15 D2
Kortrijk (Courtrai) B ... 5 D1
Kotten NL 7 E3
Kranenburg D 7 D3
Krefeld D 7 D2
Kreuztal D 15 F4
Krimpen
  aan den IJssel NL 6 B3
Kruiningen NL 5 F2
Kusel D 15 E1
Kyllburg D 15 D2

L

L'Aber-Wrac'h F 8 B3
L'Aigle F 11 D1
L'Aiguillon F 24 A3
L'Alpe-d'Huez F 35 D2
L'Arbresle F 34 A4
L'Argentière-
  la-Bessée F 35 D1
L'Echalp F 35 E1
L'Escarène F 42 C3
L'Isle-Adam F 12 B1
L'Isle-de-Noé F 37 F3
L'Isle-en-Dodon F 38 B3
L'Isle-Jourdain F 38 B4
L'Isle-Jourdain F 25 D3
L'Isle-sur-la-Sorgue F .. 41 D3
L'Isle-sur-le-Doubs F ... 29 D4
L'Ile-Bouchard F 18 C1
La Bassée F 12 C4
La Bastide
  de-Sérou F 38 B3
La Bastide-
  Puylaurent F 33 E2
La Bâtie-Neuve F 35 D1
La Baule F 17 D3
La Bazoche-Gouet F ... 19 D3
La Belle Etoile F 21 D3
La Bérarde F 35 D2
La Bourboule F 32 C4
La Brède F 30 C3
La Bresse F 22 C1
La Brillanne F 41 E3
La Canourgue F 33 D2
La Capelle F 13 E3
La Capte F 41 F1
La Cavalerie F 39 F4
La Celle-Dunoise F 26 A2
La Chaise-Dieu F 33 E3
La Chambre F 35 D3
La Chapelle F 27 F1
La Chapelle-
  d'Angillon F 20 A1
La Chapelle-
  en-Vercors F 34 B2
La Chapelle-Glain F ... 17 F3
La Charité-
  sur-Loire F 26 C4
La Chartre F 19 D2
La Châtaigneraie F 24 B4
La Châtre F 26 B3
La Chaux-
  de-Fonds CH 29 D3
La Ciotat F 41 E2
La Clayette F 27 E2
La Clusaz F 35 D4
La Cluse F 28 B1
La Cluse-et-Mijoux F .. 28 C2
La Coquille F 25 E1
La Côte-St-André F ... 34 B3
La Courtine F 26 B1
La Croisière F 25 E2
La Croix-Valmer F 42 B2
La Croixille F 18 A4
La Cure F 28 C2
La Fère F 13 D2
La Ferté-Bernard F 19 D3
La Ferté-Gaucher F ... 20 C4
La Ferté-Macé F 10 C1
La Ferté-Milon F 12 C1
La Ferté-
  sous-Jouarre F 12 C1
La Ferté-St-Aubin F ... 19 F2
La Ferté-Vidame F 11 E1
La Flèche F 18 C3
La Flotte F 24 A3
La Gacilly F 17 E3
La Garde-Freinet F ... 42 B2
La Grand-Combe F ... 33 E1
La Grande-Motte F ... 40 B3
La Grave F 35 D2
La Guerche F 26 C3
La Guerche-
  de-Bretagne F 18 A3

La Haye-du-Puits F 10 B3
La Hutte F 18 C4
La Javie F 42 B4
La Jonquera E 39 E1
La Loupe F 19 E4
La Louvière B 13 E4
La Machine F 27 D3
La Malène F 33 D1
La Maucarrière F 24 C4
La Molina E 38 C1
La Mongie F 37 E2
La Mothe-Achard F ... 17 E1
La Motte-
  Chalancon F 34 B1
La Mure F 34 C2
La Napoule-Plage F ... 42 B2
La Neuve-Lyre F 11 E1
La Neuveville CH 29 E3
La Pacaudière F 27 D1
La Pallice F 24 A3
La Palmyre F 24 A2
La Palud-
  sur-Verdon F 42 A3
La Petite-Pierre F 23 D3
La Plagne F 35 E3
La Pobla de Segur E ... 38 A1
La Réole F 31 D3
La Roche-Bernard F ... 17 D3
La Roche-Chalais F ... 31 D4
La Roche-
  en-Ardenne B 14 B3
La Roche-Posay F 25 E4
La Roche-
  sur-Foron F 35 D4
La Roche-sur-Yon F ... 17 E1
La Rochefoucauld F ... 25 D2
La Rochelle F 24 A3
La Rochette F 35 D3
La Roque-Gageac F ... 31 F3
La Roquebrussanne F .. 41 E2
La Salvetat F 32 B1
La Salvetat-
  sur-Agout F 39 E3
La Seu d'Urgell E 38 B1
La Seyne F 41 E2
La Souterraine F 25 F2
La Suze-sur-Sarthe F .. 18 C3
La Thuile F 35 E3
La Tour-du-Pin F 34 C3
La Tranche-sur-Mer F . 24 A3
La Tremblade F 24 A2
La Trimouille F 25 E3
La Trinité F 16 C3
La Trinité-Porhoët F .. 9 D1
La Turbie F 42 C3
La Voulte-
  sur-Rhône F 34 A2
La Wantzenau F 23 E3
Laarbruch D 7 D2
Labastide-
  d'Armagnac F 30 C2
Labastide-Murat F 32 A2
Labenne F 30 A1
Labouheyre F 30 B2
Labrit F 30 C2
Lacanau F 30 B4
Lacanau-Océan F 30 B4
Lacapelle-Marival F ... 32 B2
Lacaune F 39 E4
Lacq F 37 D3
Ladbergen D 7 F3
Ladon F 20 B2
Laferté F 22 A1
Laffrey F 34 C2
Lafrançaise F 31 E1
Lagnieu F 34 C4
Lagny F 12 C1
Lagrasse F 39 D2
Laguépie F 32 B1
Laguiole F 32 C2
Lahnstein D 15 E3
Lahr D 23 E2
Laignes F 21 D2
Laissac F 32 C2
Lalinde F 31 E3
Lalouvesc F 34 A3
Lamalou-les-Bains F ... 39 E3

Lamarche F 22 B2
Lamarque F 30 C4
Lamastre F 34 A2
Lamballe F 9 E2
Lambesc F 41 D3
Lambrecht D 23 E4
Lamotte-Beuvron F ... 19 F2
Lampaul-Plouarzel F .. 8 A2
Lamure-
  sur-Azergues F 27 E1
Landau D 23 E4
Landerneau F 8 B2
Landévennec F 8 B2
Landivisiau F 8 B2
Landivy F 10 B1
Landrecies F 13 E3
Landstuhl D 15 E1
Langeac F 33 D3
Langeais F 18 C2
Langenfeld D 7 E1
Langenhahn D 15 F3
Langenthal CH 29 E2
Langnau
  im Emmental CH 29 F2
Langogne F 33 E2
Langoiran F 30 C3
Langon F 30 C3
Langres F 21 F2
Lanmeur F 8 C2
Lannemezan F 37 E2
Lannilis F 8 B3
Lannion F 8 C2
Lanouaille F 31 F4
Lanslebourg-
  Mont-Cenis F 35 E2
Lantosque F 42 C3
Lanvollon F 9 D2
Lanzo Torinese I 35 F2
Laon F 13 D2
Lapalisse F 27 D2
Laplume F 31 D2
Lapoutroie F 23 D2
Laqueuille F 32 C4
Laragne-Montéglin F . 41 E4
Larche F 32 A3
Larche F 42 B4
Largentière F 33 E1
Larmor F 16 C4
Larochette L 14 C2
Laroque-des-Arcs F ... 31 F2
Laroquebrou F 32 B3
Larrau F 36 C2
Laruns F 37 D2
Las Campanas F 36 B2
Lassay F 10 C1
Lassigny F 12 C2
Lathen D 3 F2
Laubrières F 18 A3
Laufen D 29 E3
Laufenburg D 29 F4
Laufenburg CH 29 F3
Laupen CH 29 E2
Laurière F 25 F2
Lausanne CH 29 D2
Lauterbourg F 23 F3
Lauterbrunnen CH ... 29 F1
Lauterecken D 15 E1
Lautrec F 39 D4
Lauwersoog NL 3 D4
Lauzerte F 31 E2
Lauzun F 31 D3
Laval F 18 B3
Lavardac F 31 D2
Lavaur F 38 C4
Lavelanet F 38 C2
Lavoûte-Chilhac F 33 D3
Lavoûte-sur-Loire F .. 33 E3
Le Bar F 30 B3
Le Barp F 30 B3
Le Beausset F 41 E2
Le Blanc F 25 E3
Le Boulou F 39 E1
Le Bourg-d'Oisans F .. 34 C2
Le Bourget F 34 C3
Le Bugue F 31 E3
Le Cap-d'Agde F 40 A2

51

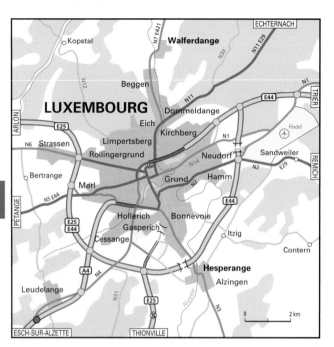

52

Le Cateau-
 Cambrésis F 13 D3
Le Catelet F 13 D3
Le Caylar F 40 A4
Le Chateau-
 d'Oléron F 24 A2
Le Châtelard F 35 D3
Le Châtelet F 26 B3
Le Chesne F 13 F2
Le Cheylard F 33 F2
Le Conquet F 8 A2
Le Creusot F 27 E3
Le Croisic F 17 D3
Le Crotoy F 12 B4
Le Donjon F 27 D2
Le Dorat F 25 E2
Le Faou F 8 B2
Le Faouët F 8 C1
Le Fossat F 38 B3
Le Grand-Bourg F 25 F2
Le Grand-Lucé F 19 D3
Le Grand-Pressigny F 25 E4
Le Grau-du-Roi F 40 B3
Le Havre F 11 D3
Le Hohwald F 23 D2
Le Lauzet-Ubaye F 42 B4
Le Lavandou F 42 A1
Le Lion-d'Angers F 18 B3
Le Locle CH 29 D3
Le Logis-du-Pin F 42 B3
Le Loroux-
 Bottereau F 17 F2
Le Louroux F 18 A3
Le Luc F 42 A2
Le Lude F 18 C2
Le Mans F 18 C3
Le Markstein F 23 D1
Le Mas-d'Azil F 38 B3
Le Mayet F 27 D1
Le Merlerault F 11 D1
Le Monastier F 33 E2
Le Monêtier-
 les-Bains F 35 D2
Le Mont-Dore F 33 D4
Le Mont-St-Michel F 10 A2
Le Montet F 26 C2
Le Muret F 30 B3

Le Muy F 42 B2
Le Neubourg F 11 E2
Le Nouvion-
 en-Thiérache F 13 E3
Le Palais F 16 C3
Le Perthus F 39 E1
Le Pin-au-Haras F 11 D1
Le Poiré-sur-Vie F 17 E1
Le Pont-
 de-Beauvoisin F 34 C3
Le Pont-de-Claix F 34 C2
Le Pontet F 24 B1
Le Portel F 4 B1
Le Pouldu F 16 C4
Le Pouzin F 34 A2
Le Puy F 33 E3
Le Quesnoy F 13 D3
Le Rabot F 19 F2
Le Rozier F 33 D1
Le Russey F 29 D3
Le Teil F 34 A1
Le Teilleul F 10 B1
Le Thillot F 22 C1
Le Touquet-
 Paris-Plage F 4 B1
Le Touvet F 34 C3
Le Trayas F 42 B2
Le Tréport F 12 A4
Le Val-André F 9 E2
Le Vaudreuil F 11 F2
Le Verdon F 24 A2
Le Vernet F 42 B4
Le Vigan F 40 B4
Le-Péage-
 de-Roussillon F 34 B3
Lebach D 15 D1
Lectoure F 31 D1
Lédignan F 40 C4
Leek NL 3 E3
Leer D 3 F3
Leerdam NL 6 B3
Leeuwarden NL 3 D3
Legden D 7 E3
Legé F 17 E1
Léguevin F 38 B4
Leiden NL 2 B1
Leissigen CH 29 F2

Lekeitio E 36 A4
Lekunberri E 36 B3
Lelystad NL 2 C2
Lembach F 23 E3
Lembeye F 37 E3
Lemmer NL 3 D3
Lempdes F 33 D3
Lempdes F 26 C1
Lencloître F 25 D4
Lenk CH 29 E1
Lens F 12 C4
Lenzkirch D 23 E1
Léon F 30 A2
Leopoldsburg B 6 B1
Lés E 37 F1
Les Abrets F 34 C3
Les Adrets F 42 B2
Les Aix-d'Angillon F 26 C4
Les Andelys F 11 F2
Les Arcs F 35 E3
Les Arcs F 42 B2
Les Baux-
 de-Provence F 41 D3
Les Cabannes F 38 C2
Les Contamines-
 Montjoie F 35 E4
Les Deux-Alpes F 35 D2
Les Diablerets CH 29 E1
Les Echarmeaux F 27 E1
Les Echelles F 34 C3
Les Epesses F 18 A1
Les Escaldes AND 38 B1
Les Essarts F 17 E1
Les Eyzies-de-Tayac F 31 E3
Les Gets F 29 D1
Les Halles F 34 A4
Les Haudères CH 35 F4
Les Hayons F 11 F3
Les Herbiers F 17 F1
Les Houches F 35 E4
Les Issambres F 42 B2
Les Laumes F 21 D1
Les Lecques F 41 E2
Les Menuires F 35 D3
Les Pieux F 10 A4
Les Planches-
 en-Montagne F 28 C2

Les Ponts-de-Cé F 18 B2
Les Riceys F 21 D2
Les Rosiers F 18 B2
Les Rousses F 28 C2
Les Sables-
 d'Olonne F 24 A4
Les Trois-Epis F 23 D2
Les Trois-Moutiers F 18 B1
Les Vans F 33 E1
Lescar F 37 D3
Lesmont F 21 E3
Lesneven F 8 B2
Lesparre-Médoc F 24 A1
Lessay F 10 B3
Lessines B 5 E1
Lestelle Bétharram F 37 E2
Letmathe D 7 F2
Leucate F 39 E2
Leuglay F 21 E2
Leuk CH 29 E1
Leukerbad CH 29 E1
Leuven (Louvain) B 6 A1
Leuze B 13 E4
Levens F 42 C3
Leverkusen D 7 E1
Levet F 26 B3
Levie F 43 a1
Levier F 28 C3
Levroux F 26 A4
Leyre E 36 C2
Leysin CH 29 D1
Lezay F 24 C3
Lézignan-Corbières F 39 E3
Lezoux F 26 C1
Libourne F 30 C4
Libramont B 14 B2
Lichtenvoorde NL 7 D3
Liège (Luik) B 14 B4
Lier B 6 A2
Liernais F 27 E4
Liestal CH 29 E1
Lieurey F 11 D2
Liffré F 17 F4
Ligneuville B 14 C3
Lignières F 26 B3
Ligny-en-Barrois F 22 A3
Ligueil F 19 D1
Lille F 5 D1
Lillebonne F 11 E3
Lillers F 4 C1
Limburg D 15 F3
Limoges F 25 E2
Limogne-
 en-Quercy F 32 A2
Limone Piemonte I 43 D3
Limonest F 34 B4
Limours F 20 A4
Limoux F 39 D2
Lingen D 3 F2
Linz D 15 E3
Lisieux F 11 D2
Lisle F 38 C4
Lisse NL 2 B2
Lit-et-Mixe F 30 A2
Livarot F 11 D2
Livernon F 32 B2
Livron F 34 A2
Lizy F 12 C1
Llançà E 39 E1
Llavorsí E 38 B2
Lles E 38 C1
Lochem NL 7 D3
Loches F 19 D1
Locmaria F 16 C3
Locmariaquer F 16 C3
Locminé F 17 D4
Locquirec F 8 C2
Locronan F 8 B1
Loctudy F 8 B1
Lodève F 40 A3
Lodosa E 36 A2
Loga D 3 F3
Lohéac F 17 E4
Lohnsfeld D 15 E1
Lokeren B 5 F2
Lombez F 38 B4
Lomme F 5 D1

Lommel B 6 B2
Londinières F 12 A3
Longeau F 21 F1
Longny-au-Perche F....... 19 D4
Longué F 18 B2
Longuyon F 14 B1
Longwy F 14 B1
Lons-le-Saunier F 28 B2
Lorcé B 14 C3
Lorch D 15 E2
Lorentzen F 23 D3
Lorgues F 42 A2
Lorient F 16 C4
Loriol-sur-Drôme F....... 34 A2
Lormes F 27 E4
Lormont F 30 C4
Lörrach D 29 F4
Lorris F 20 B2
Lorup D 3 F3
Los Arcos E 36 A2
Losheim D 15 D1
Losheim D 14 C3
Lossburg D 23 F2
Loudéac F 9 D1
Loudes F 33 E3
Loudun F 18 C1
Loué F 18 C3
Louhans F 28 B2
Loulay F 24 B3
Lourdes F 37 E2
Louvain (Leuven) B 6 A1
Louviers F 11 E2
Lubersac F 32 A4
Luc-en-Diois F 34 B1
Luc-sur-Mer F 10 C3
Lucenay F........................... 27 E3
Luçon F 24 B4
Lüdenscheid D..................... 7 F1
Lüdinghausen D 7 F2
Ludwigshafen D.................. 15 F1
Luigny F 19 E3
Luik (Liège) B................... 14 B4
Lumbier E 36 B2
Lumbres F 4 C1
Lummen B............................. 6 B1
Lunas F 39 F3
Lunel F 40 B3
Lünen D 7 F2
Lunéville F 22 C3
Lungern CH 29 F2
Lünne D 3 F1
Lurcy-Lévis F 26 C3
Lure F 29 D4
Lureuil F 25 E3
Luri F 43 b3
Lus-la-Croix-Haute F ... 34 C1
Lusignan F 25 D3
Lusigny F 21 D3
Lussac-
  les-Châteaux F........... 25 E3
Lussan F 40 C4
Luxembourg L 14 C2
Luxeuil-les-Bains F 22 B1
Luz-St-Sauveur F............ 37 E2
Luzarches F 12 B1
Luzy F 27 E3
Lydd GB 4 A2
Lyon F 34 B4
Lyons-la-Forêt F 12 A2
Lyss CH 29 E3

M

Maaseik B 6 C1
Maasmechelen B................. 6 C1
Maassluis NL....................... 6 A3
Maastricht NL 6 C1
Machault F 13 E1
Mâchecoul F 17 E2
Mâcon F 27 F2
Made NL 6 B3
Magescq F 30 A2
Magnac-Laval F 25 E2

Magny-en-Vexin F........... 12 A2
Maîche F 29 D3
Maidstone GB 4 A3
Mailly-le-Camp F 21 D3
Maintenon F 19 F4
Mainz D 15 F2
Malaucène F 41 D4
Malbuisson F 28 C2
Maldegem B 5 E2
Maldon GB 4 A4
Malesherbes F 20 B3
Malestroit F 17 D4
Malicorne F 18 C3
Malines (Mechelen) B..... 6 A1
Malmédy B 14 C3
Malo-les-Bains F 4 C2
Mamers F 19 D4
Mandelieu F 42 B2
Manderscheid D 15 D2
Mannheim D....................... 15 F1
Manosque F 41 E3
Mansle F 24 C2
Mantes F 12 A1
Manzat F 26 C1
Marans F 24 B3
Marboz F 28 B2
Marchaux F 28 C3
Marche-
  en-Famenne B 14 B3
Marcheprime F 30 B3
Marciac F 37 E3
Marcigny F 27 E2
Marcilla E 36 B1
Marcillac-Vallon F 32 B2
Marcillat F 26 B2
Marcilly-le-Hayer F 21 D3
Marckolsheim F................ 23 D2
Marennes F 24 A2
Mareuil F 25 D1
Mareuil F 24 B4
Margate GB 4 B3
Maria Laach D 15 E3
Marignane F 41 D2
Marigny-le-Châtel F....... 21 D3
Marines F 12 B2
Maringues F 26 C1
Marl D 7 E2
Marle F 13 D2
Marlenheim F 23 D3
Marmande F 31 D3
Marmoutier F 23 D3
Marnay F 28 C3
Marquion F 13 D3
Marquise F 4 B2
Marseillan F 40 A3
Marseillan-Plage F.......... 40 A3
Marseille F 41 D2
Marseille-
  en-Beauvaisis F......... 12 B2
Martel F 32 A3
Martelange B 14 B2
Martigné-Ferchaud F...... 17 F3
Martigny CH 35 E4
Martigues F 41 D2
Marvejols F 33 D2
Marxzell D 23 F3
Masevaux F 22 C1
Massat F 38 B2
Massay F 26 B4
Masseube F 38 A4
Massiac F 33 D3
Matha F 24 C2
Mathay F 29 D3
Matignon F 9 E2
Matour F 27 F2
Maubeuge F 13 E3
Maubourguet F 37 E3
Mauléon F 18 A1
Mauléon-Licharre F....... 36 C3
Maulévrier F 18 A1
Maupertus-sur-Mer F.... 10 B4
Maure F 17 E4
Mauriac F 32 C3
Mauron F 17 E4
Maurs F 32 B2
Maury F 39 D2
Mauvezin F 38 B4

Mauzé-
  sur-le-Mignon F 24 B3
Mayen D 15 E3
Mayenne F 18 B4
Mayet F 18 C3
Mazamet F 39 D3
Mazères F 38 C3
Meaux F 12 C1
Mechelen (Malines) B..... 6 A1
Mechernich D 15 D3
Medemblik NL 2 C3
Megève F 35 E4
Mehun-sur-Yèvre F 26 B4
Meijel NL 6 C2
Meinerzhagen D 7 F1
Meiringen CH 29 F2
Meisenheim D 15 E1
Mélisey F 22 C1
Melle F 24 C3
Melun F 20 B4
Menat F 26 C2
Mendavia E 36 A2
Mende F 33 D2
Menden D 7 F2
Menen B 5 D1
Mens F 34 C2
Menthon F 35 D4
Menton F 42 C3
Meppel NL 3 D2
Meppen D 3 F2
Mer F 19 E2
Merdrignac F 9 E1
Méréville F 20 A3
Méribel F 35 D3
Merligen CH 29 F2
Mersch L 14 C2
Mersch D 7 D1
Méru F 12 B2
Mervans F 28 B2
Méry F 21 D3
Merzig D 15 D1
Meschers-
  sur-Gironde F 24 B2
Meslay F 18 B3
Mesnil-Val F 12 A4
Mesvres F 27 E3
Metabief F 28 C2
Méteren F 5 D1
Mettet B 13 F3
Mettingen D 7 F3
Mettlach D 15 D1
Mettmann D 7 E1
Metz F 22 C4
Metzervisse F 14 C1
Meulan F 12 A1
Meung-sur-Loire F 19 E2
Meximieux F 34 B4
Meymac F 32 B4
Meyrargues F 41 E3
Meyrueis F 33 D1
Meyzieu F 34 B4
Mèze F 40 A3
Mézel F 42 A3
Mézières F 25 E2
Mézières-
  en-Brenne F 25 E4
Mézilhac F 33 F2
Mézin F 31 D2
Middelburg NL 5 E3
Middelharnis NL 6 A3
Middelkerke-Bad B 5 D2
Midsland NL 2 C4
Miélan F 37 F3
Migennes F 20 C2
Mijoux F 28 C1
Millas F 39 D1
Millau F 32 C1
Mimizan F 30 A2
Mimizan-Plage F 30 A2
Mindin F 17 D2
Miramar F 42 B2
Miramas F 41 D3
Mirambeau F 24 B1
Miramont-
  de-Guyenne F 31 D3
Mirande F 37 F3
Mirebeau F 25 D4

Mirebeau F 28 B4
Mirecourt F 22 B2
Mirepoix F 38 C3
Modane F 35 E2
Modave B 14 B3
Moers D 7 D2
Moirans F 34 C3
Moirans-
  en-Montagne F 28 B2
Moissac F 31 E1
Mol B 6 B2
Molare I 43 E4
Molières F 31 F2
Molliens F 12 B3
Moloy F 28 A4
Molsheim F 23 D2
Monaco MC 42 C2
Moncalieri I........................ 35 F2
Mönchengladbach D 7 D1
Moncontour F 9 D1
Moncoutant F 24 C4
Mondorf-les-Bains L 14 C1
Mondoubleau F 19 D3
Mondovì I 43 D4
Mondragón E 36 A3
Monestier-
  de-Clermont F............ 34 C2
Monflanquin F 31 E2
Monistrol-d'Allier F........ 33 E3
Monistrol-sur-Loire F... 33 F3
Monnickendam NL 2 C2
Monpazier F 31 E3
Monplaisir F 19 D3
Monreal E 36 B2
Mons (Bergen) B 13 E4
Monschau D 14 C3
Monségur F 31 D3
Monsheim D........................ 15 F1
Mont-de-Marsan F........... 30 B2
Mont-Louis F 38 C1
Mont-sous-Vaudrey F 28 B3
Montabaur D 15 F3
Montagnac F 40 A3
Montaigu F 17 E2
Montaigu-
  de-Quercy F 31 E2
Montaigut F 26 C2
Montalivet-
  les-Bains F 24 A1
Montana CH 29 E1
Montaren F 40 C4
Montargis F 20 B2
Montastruc
  la-Conseillère F 38 C4
Montauban F 31 F1
Montbard F 21 D1
Montbazens F 32 B2
Montbazon F 19 D2
Montbéliard F 29 D4
Montbenoît F 29 D3
Montbonnot F 34 C2
Montbrison F 33 F4
Montbron F 25 D1
Montbrun-les-Bains F 41 E4
Montceau-
  les-Mines F 27 E2
Montcornet F 13 E2
Montcuq F 31 E2
Montdidier F 12 C2
Monte-Carlo MC 42 C2
Montebourg F 10 B3
Montélimar F 34 A1
Montendre F 24 B1
Montereau F 20 C3
Montesquieu-
  Volvestre F 38 B3
Montesquiou F 37 F3
Montfaucon-
  en-Velay F 33 F3
Montfort F 30 B1
Montfort F 17 E4
Montfort F 12 A1
Montgenèvre F 35 E2
Montgiscard F 38 C3
Montguyon F 31 D4
Monthermé F 13 F2
Monthey CH........................ 29 D1

53

Monthois F	13 F1	Mouy F	12 B2
Monthureaux-		Mouzon F	14 A2
sur-Saône F	22 B2	Much D	15 E4
Montier-en-Der F	21 E3	Mugron F	30 B1
Montignac F	31 F3	Mülheim D	15 D2
Montigny-le-Roi F	22 A2	Mülheim D	7 E2
Montigny-sur-Aube F	21 E2	Mulhouse F	29 E4
Montivilliers F	11 D3	Müllheim D	23 D1
Montlieu-la-Garde F	24 B1	Münsingen CH	29 E2
Montluçon F	26 B2	Münster CH	29 F1
Montluel F	34 B4	Münster F	23 D2
Montmarault F	26 C2	Münster D	7 F3
Montmédy F	14 B2	Münstertal D	23 E1
Montmélian F	35 D3	Mur-de-Barrez F	32 C2
Montmirail F	19 D3	Mur-de-Bretagne F	9 D1
Montmirail F	21 D4	Murat F	32 C3
Montmirey F	28 B3	Murato I	43 b3
Montmoreau-		Murat-sur-Vèbre F	39 E3
St-Cybard F	24 C1	Muret F	38 B3
Montmorillon F	25 E3	Muro F	43 a3
Montmort F	21 D4	Mürren CH	29 F1
Montoire-		Murten CH	29 E2
sur-le-Loir F	19 D2	Musselkanaal NL	3 E3
Montpellier F	40 B3	Mussidan F	31 D4
Montpezat F	31 F2	Mussy F	21 E2
Montpon-		Mutterstadt D	15 F1
Ménestérol F	31 D4	Muzillac F	17 D3
Montpont-			
en-Bresse F	28 A2		
Montréal F	31 D1		
Montréal F	39 D3		
Montréjeau F	37 F2		
Montrésor F	19 D1		
Montret F	28 A2	N	
Montreuil F	4 B1		
Montreuil-			
aux-Lions F	12 C1	Naarden NL	2 C2
Montreuil-Bellay F	18 B1	Nadrin F	14 B3
Montreux CH	29 D1	Nagold D	23 F2
Montrevel F	28 A2	Nailloux F	38 C3
Montrichard F	19 D2	Najac F	32 B1
Montrond-les-Bains F	33 F4	Nalzen F	38 C2
Monts-s-Guesnes F	18 C1	Namen B	14 A4
Montsalvy F	32 C2	Nancy F	22 B3
Montsauche-		Nangis F	20 C3
les-Settons F	27 E4	Nans-les-Pins F	41 E2
Montsoreau F	18 C2	Nant F	40 A4
Montsûrs F	18 B4	Nantes F	17 E2
Moordorf D	3 F4	Nanteuil-	
Morbach D	15 D2	le-Haudouin F	12 C1
Morcenx F	30 B2	Nantiat F	25 E2
Mordelles F	17 E4	Nantua F	28 B1
Morestel F	34 C3	Narbonne F	39 E2
Moretta I	35 F1	Narbonne-Plage F	39 E2
Moreuil F	12 C3	Nasbinals F	33 D2
Morez F	28 C2	Nassau D	15 F3
Morgat F	8 B2	Navarrenx F	37 D3
Morges CH	29 D2	Navilly F	28 B3
Morgex I	35 E3	Neauvic F	31 E4
Morgins CH	29 D1	Neede D	7 E3
Morhange F	22 C3	Neermoor D	3 F3
Morlaàs F	37 E3	Neheim-Hüsten D	7 F2
Morlaix F	8 C2	Nemours F	20 B3
Mormant F	20 C4	Nérac F	31 D2
Morosaglia F	43 b2	Néris-les-Bains F	26 B2
Mortagne-		Nérondes F	26 C3
au-Perche F	19 D4	Nervi I	43 F4
Mortagne-sur-Sèvre F	17 F1	Nes NL	3 D4
Mortain F	10 B1	Nesle F	12 C3
Morteau F	29 D3	Nettancourt F	21 F4
Mortrée F	11 D1	Nettetal D	7 D2
Morzine F	29 D1	Neu-Moresnet B	14 C4
Mouchard F	28 C3	Neuchâtel CH	29 D3
Moudon CH	29 D2	Neudorf D	23 F4
Mougins F	42 B2	Neuenburg D	23 D1
Mouliherne F	18 C2	Neuenbürg D	23 F3
Moulins F	27 D2	Neuenhaus D	3 E2
Moulins-Engilbert F	27 E3	Neuf-Brisach F	23 D1
Moulins-la-Marche F	11 D1	Neufchâteau F	22 B2
Moustiers-		Neufchâteau B	14 B2
Ste-Marie F	42 A3	Neufchâtel F	13 E2
Mouthe F	28 C2	Neufchâtel-en-Bray F	12 A3
Mouthier F	28 C3	Neuhausen	
Mouthoumet F	39 D2	am Rheinfall CH	23 F1
Moutier CH	29 E3	Neuillé Port-Pierre F	19 D2
Moûtiers F	35 D3	Neuilly-l'Évêque F	22 A2
Moutiers F	24 A4	Neuilly-St-Front F	13 D1
		Neung-sur-Beuvron F	19 E2
		Neunkirchen D	15 D1

Neuss D	7 D1		
Neustadt D	23 E1		
Neustadt an der			
Weinstrasse D	23 F4		
Neuves-Maisons F	22 B3		
Neuvic F	32 C4		
Neuville F	34 B4		
Neuville F	25 D4		
Neuville-aux-Bois F	20 A3		
Neuvy F	26 A3		
Neuvy-			
sur-Barangeon F	20 A1		
Neuwied D	15 E3		
Nevers F	27 D3		
New Romney GB	4 A2		
Nexon F	25 E1		
Nice F	42 C2		
Niederbronn-			
les-Bains F	23 E3		
Niederkrüchten D	7 D1		
Nieppe F	5 D1		
Nierstein D	15 F2		
Nieuil F	25 D2		
Nieuweschans NL	3 F3		
Nieuwpoort B	5 D2		
Nijkerk NL	2 C1		
Nijmegen NL	6 C3		
Nijverdal NL	3 D2		
Nîmes F	40 C3		
Ninove B	5 E1		
Niort F	24 C3		
Nitry F	21 D1		
Nivelles B	13 F4		
Nizza Monferrato I	43 E4		
Noailles F	12 B2		
Noain E	36 B2		
Noeux F	12 C4		
Nogaro F	37 E4		
Nogent F	21 F2		
Nogent-le-Roi F	19 F4		
Nogent-le-Rotrou F	19 D4		
Nogent-sur-Seine F	20 C3		
Nohfelden D	15 D1		
Noirétable F	33 E4		
Noirmoutier-			
en-l'Île F	17 D2		
Nolay F	27 F3		
Nomeny F	22 C3		
Nomexy F	22 C2		
Nonancourt F	11 E1		
Nonant-le-Pin F	11 D1		
Nontron F	25 D1		
Nonza F	43 b3		
Noordwijk			
aan Zee NL	2 B2		
Nordausques F	4 C2		
Norddeich D	3 F4		
Norden D	3 F4		
Norderney D	3 F4		
Nordhorn D	3 E2		
Norg NL	3 E3		
Nort F	17 E3		
Nottuln D	7 F3		
Nouan-le-Fuzelier F	19 F2		
Nouans-			
les-Fontaines F	19 D1		
Nouvion F	12 B4		
Noves F	41 D3		
Novi Ligure I	43 F4		
Novion-Porcien F	13 E2		
Noyant F	18 C2		
Noyers F	21 D1		
Noyers-sur-Jabron F	41 E4		
Noyon F	12 C2		
Nozay F	17 E3		
Nozeroy F	28 C2		
Nuits-St-Georges F	28 A3		
Nunspeet NL	3 D2		
Nürburg D	15 D3		
Nyon CH	28 C1		
Nyons F	34 B1		

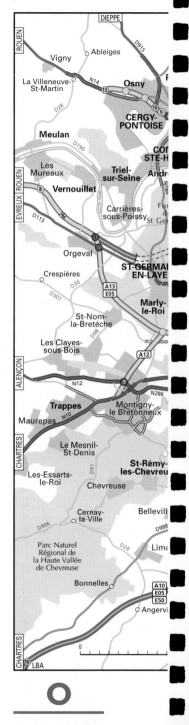

Oberhausen D................ 7 E2

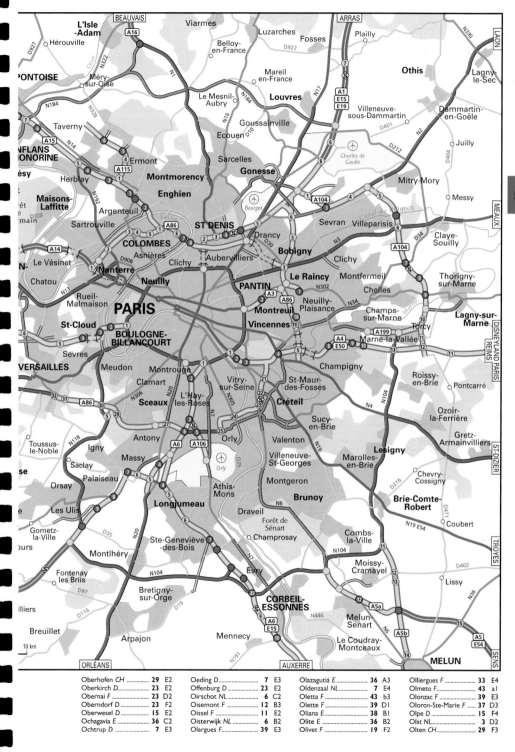

Oberhofen *CH*	29	E2	Oeding *D*	7	E3	Olazagutía *E*	36	A3
Oberkirch *D*	23	E2	Offenburg *D*	23	E2	Oldenzaal *NL*	7	E4
Obernai *F*	23	D2	Oirschot *NL*	6	C2	Oletta *F*	43	b3
Oberndorf *D*	23	F2	Oisemont *F*	12	B3	Olette *F*	39	DI
Oberwesel *D*	15	E2	Oissel *F*	11	E2	Oliana *F*	38	BI
Ochagavia *E*	36	C2	Oisterwijk *NL*	6	B2	Olite *E*	36	B2
Ochtrup *D*	7	E3	Olargues *F*	39	E3	Olivet *F*	19	F2

Olliergues *F*	33	E4
Olmeto *F*	43	a I
Olonzac *F*	39	E3
Oloron-Ste-Marie *F*	37	D3
Olpe *D*	15	F4
Olst *NL*	3	D2
Olten *CH*	29	F3

Ommen NL	3	D2	Payrac F	32	A3	Poncin F	28	B1	Primel-Trégastel F	8	C3
Ondarroa E	36	A4	Péaule F	17	D3	Pons F	24	B2	Primstal D	15	D1
Onnaing F	13	D4	Pegli I	43	F4	Pont-à-Mousson F	22	B4	Privas F	34	A2
Oostburg NL	5	E2	Peira-Cava F	42	C3	Pont-Audemer F	11	E2	Profondeville B	14	A3
Oostende B	5	D2	Pellegrue F	31	D3	Pont-Aven F	8	B1	Pronsfeld D	14	C3
Oosterbeek NL	6	C3	Pentrez-Plage F	8	B2	Pont-Croix F	8	B1	Propriano F	43	a1
Oostérend F	2	C4	Peralta F	36	A1	Pont-d'Ain F	28	B1	Provins F	20	C3
Oosterhout NL	6	B3	Percy F	10	B2	Pont-de-Briques F	4	B1	Prüm D	15	D3
Oosterwolde NL	3	D3	Périers F	10	B3	Pont-de-Dore F	27	D1	Prunete F	43	b2
Oostmalle B	6	B2	Périgueux F	31	E4	Pont-de-l'Arche F	11	E2	Puente la Reina E	36	B2
Ootmarsum NL	3	E2	Perkpolder NL	5	F2	Pont-de-Roide F	29	D3	Puffendorf D	7	D1
Opladen D	7	E1	Pernes F	41	D4	Pont-de-Salars F	32	C1	Puget-sur-Argens F	42	B2
Oppenau D	23	E2	Péronne F	12	C3	Pont-de-Vaux F	28	A2	Puget-Théniers F	42	B3
Oppenheim D	15	F2	Pérouges F	34	B4	Pont-en-Royans F	34	B2	Puget-Ville F	41	F2
Oraison F	41	E3	Perpignan F	39	E1	Pont-l'Abbé F	8	B1	Puigcerda E	38	C1
Orange F	41	D4	Perros-Guirec F	9	D3	Pont-l'Evêque F	11	D2	Puiseaux F	20	B3
Orbassano I	35	F2	Pertuis F	41	E3	Pont-Réan F	17	E4	Puivert F	38	C2
Orbe CH	29	D2	Péruwelz B	13	E4	Pont-Scorff F	16	C4	Purmerend NL	2	B2
Orbec F	11	D2	Pesmes F	28	B3	Pont-St-Esprit F	41	D4	Putanges-		
Orbey F	23	D2	Pétange L	14	B1	Pont-St-Vincent F	22	B3	Pont-Ecrepin F	10	C1
Orchies F	13	D4	Petreto-Bicchisano F	43	a1	Pont-sur-Yonne F	20	C3	Puttelange F	23	D4
Orcières F	35	D1	Peyrat-le-Chateaux F	25	F1	Pontacq F	37	E3	Putten NL	2	C1
Ordino AND	38	B2	Peyrehorade F	36	C4	Pontailler-sur-Saône F	28	B3	Puy de Dôme F	26	C1
Orgelet F	28	B2	Peyrolles F	41	E3	Pontarion F	26	A2	Puy-Guillaume F	27	D1
Orgeval F	12	B1	Peyruis F	41	F3	Pontarlier F	28	C2	Puy-l'Evêque F	31	E2
Orgon F	41	D3	Pézenas F	40	A3	Pontaubault F	10	A2	Puylaurens F	39	D3
Orio E	36	A3	Pforzheim D	23	F3	Pontaumur F	26	B1	Pyla-sur-Mer F	30	B3
Orléans F	19	F2	Phalsbourg F	23	D3	Pontcharra F	35	D3			
Orly F	20	B4	Philippeville B	13	F3	Pontchartrain F	12	A1			
Ornans F	28	C3	Piana F	43	a2	Pontchâteau F	17	E3			
Oron-la-Ville CH	29	D2	Piana Crixia I	43	E4	Ponte-Leccia F	43	b2			
Orscholz D	14	C1	Picquigny F	12	B3	Pontedecimo I	43	F4			
Orsières CH	35	F4	Piedicroce F	43	b2	Pontgibaud F	26	C1			
Orthez F	37	D3	Pierre-Buffière F	25	E1	Pontigny F	20	C2			
Ospedaletti I	43	D3	Pierre-de-Bresse F	28	B3	Pontivy F	9	D1	Quarré-les-Tombes F	27	E4
Oss NL	6	C3	Pierrefitte F	22	A4	Pontlevoy F	19	E2	Questembert F	17	D3
Ostbevern D	7	F3	Pierrefitte-Nestalas F	37	E2	Pontoise F	12	B1	Quettehou F	10	B3
Osthofen D	15	F1	Pierrefonds F	12	C2	Pontorson F	10	A1	Quiberon F	16	C3
Ostiz E	36	B3	Pierrefort F	32	C3	Pontrieux F	9	D2	Quillan F	39	D2
Otterbach D	15	E1	Pierrelatte F	34	A1	Pontvallain F	18	C3	Quimper F	8	B1
Otterlo NL	6	C3	Pierroton F	30	B3	Poperinge B	5	D1	Quimperlé F	16	C4
Ottweiler D	15	D1	Pilat-Plage F	30	B3	Pornic F	17	D2	Quinéville F	10	B3
Oucques F	19	E2	Pinerolo I	35	E1	Pornichet F	17	D3	Quingey F	28	C3
Oud Beijerland NL	6	A3	Piney F	21	E3	Porquerolles F	41	F1	Quintin F	9	D2
Ouddorp NL	5	F3	Pino F	43	b3	Porrentruy CH	29	E3	Quissac F	40	B4
Oude-Pekela NL	3	E3	Pinols F	33	D3	Port-Barcarès F	39	E2			
Oudenaarde B	5	E1	Pionsat F	26	B2	Port-Camargue F	40	B3			
Ouistreham F	10	C3	Pipriac F	17	E3	Port-Cros F	42	A1			
Oulx I	35	E2	Piriac-sur-Mer F	17	D3	Port-de-Bouc F	41	D2			
Oust F	38	B2	Pirmasens D	23	E4	Port-en-Bessin F	10	C3			
Ouzouer-le-Marché F	19	E3	Pirou-Plage F	10	A3	Port-Grimaud F	42	B2	Raalte NL	3	D2
Ovada I	43	E4	Pissos F	30	B3	Port-la-Nouvelle F	39	E2	Rabastens F	38	C4
Overath D	15	E4	Pithiviers F	20	A3	Port-Leucate F	39	E2	Rabastens-		
Oyonnax F	28	B1	Plabennec F	8	B2	Port-Louis F	16	C4	de-Bigorre F	37	E3
			Plaisance F	37	E3	Port-Manech F	16	B4	Racconigi I	35	F1
			Plancoët F	9	E2	Port-Navalo F	16	C3	Radevormwald D	7	E1
			Pleaux F	32	B3	Port-St-Louis-			Raesfeld D	7	E2
			Plélan-le-Grand F	17	E4	du-Rhône F	40	C2	Rambervillers F	22	C2
			Plestin-les-Grèves F	8	C2	Port-Ste-Marie F	31	D2	Rambouillet F	19	F4
			Plettenberg D	7	F1	Port-sur-Saône F	22	B1	Ramsgate GB	4	B3
			Pleumartin F	25	E4	Port-Vendres F	39	E1	Ramstein D	15	E1
Pacy-sur-Eure F	11	F1	Pleyben F	8	B2	Portbail F	10	A3	Randan F	26	C1
Paesana I	35	E1	Ploërmel F	17	D4	Portbou F	39	E1	Rânes F	10	C1
Pagny F	22	B4	Plombières-			Porticcio F	43	a2	Raon-l'Etape F	22	C2
Paimboeuf F	17	E2	les-Bains F	22	C2	Porto F	43	a2	Raron CH	29	F1
Paimpol F	9	D2	Plonéour Lanvern F	8	B1	Porto-Vecchio F	43	b1	Rastatt D	23	F3
Paladru F	34	C3	Plouaret F	8	C2	Portofino I	43	F3	Ratingen D	7	E2
Palavas-les-Flots F	40	B3	Plouay F	16	C4	Pouancé F	18	A3	Raversijde B	5	D2
Paliseul B	14	B2	Ploubalay F	9	E2	Pougues-les-Eaux F	26	C4	Rayleigh GB	4	A4
Pamiers F	38	C3	Ploudalmézeau F	8	B3	Pouilly F	26	C4	Rayol F	42	A1
Pamplona/Iruñea E	36	B2	Plouescat F	8	B3	Pouilly-en-Auxois F	27	F4	Réalmont F	39	D4
Panassac F	38	A4	Plougasnou F	8	C2	Pouyastruc F	37	E3	Rebais F	20	C4
Papenburg D	3	F3	Plouguenast F	9	D1	Pouzauges F	18	A1	Recey-sur-Ource F	21	E1
Paray-le-Monial F	27	E2	Plouha F	9	D2	Pradelles F	33	E2	Recke D	7	F4
Parentis-en-Born F	30	B3	Plouigneau F	8	C2	Prades F	39	D1	Recklinghausen D	7	E2
Paris F	12	B1	Plouray F	8	C1	Prahecq F	24	C3	Recologne F	28	C3
Parkeston Quay GB	4	B4	Plozévet F	8	B1	Pralognan-			Redon F	17	E3
Parthenay F	24	C4	Pluvigner F	16	C4	la-Vanoise F	35	E3	Rees D	7	D3
Partinello F	43	a2	Podensac F	30	C3	Prats-de-Mollo-			Reignier F	28	C1
Pas de la Casa AND	38	C1	Poeldijk NL	6	A4	la-Preste F	39	D1	Reims F	13	E1
Pas-en-Artois F	12	C4	Poissons F	21	F3	Prauthoy F	21	F1	Reinach CH	29	F3
Patay F	19	E4	Poitiers F	25	D3	Pré St-Didier I	35	E3	Reinsfeld D	15	D2
Pau F	37	D3	Poix F	12	B3	Pré-en-Pail F	10	C1	Reken D	7	E3
Pauillac F	24	B1	Poix-Terron F	13	F2	Précy-sous-Thil F	27	E4	Remagen D	15	E3
Paulhaguet F	33	D3	Poligny F	28	B2	Prémery F	27	D4	Rémalard F	19	D4
Pavilly F	11	E3	Pompaples CH	29	D2	Pressac F	25	D2			
Payerne CH	29	D2	Pompey F	22	B3	Preuilly-sur-Claise F	25	E4			

P

Q

R

Remich L	14	C1	Rohrbach-			Saerbeck D	7	F3
Remiremont F	22	C2	lès-Bitche F	23	D4	Saeul L	14	C2
Remouchamps B	14	C3	Roisel F	13	D3	Sagone F	43	a2
Remoulins F	40	C4	Rolle CH	28	C2	Saignelégier CH	29	E3
Remscheid D	7	E1	Romans-sur-Isère F	34	B2	Saillagouse F	38	C1
Rémuzat F	34	B1	Rombas F	22	C4	Saillans F	34	B2
Renaison F	27	D1	Romilly-sur-Seine F	21	D3	Sains F	13	D3
Renaix (Ronse) B	5	E1	Romont CH	29	D2	St-Affrique F	39	E4
Renchen D	23	E3	Romorantin-			St-Agnant F	24	B2
Renkum NL	6	C3	Lanthenay F	19	E1	St-Agrève F	33	F2
Rennerod D	15	F3	Roncal E	36	C2	St-Aignan F	18	A3
Rennes F	17	E3	Roncesvalles E	36	C3	St-Aignan F	19	E1
Rentería E	36	B3	Ronchamp F	29	D4	St-Alban F	33	D2
Réquista F	32	B1	Ronse (Renaix) B	5	E1	St-Amand-		
Ressons F	12	C2	Roodeschool NL	3	E4	en-Puisaye F	20	B1
Rethel F	13	E2	Roosendaal NL	6	A2	St-Amand-les-Eaux F	13	D4
Retiers F	17	F3	Roquebillière F	42	C3	St-Amand-Longpré F	19	D2
Retournac F	33	E3	Roquebrune-			St-Amand-		
Reuilly F	26	B4	Cap-Martin F	42	C3	Montrond F	26	B3
Reusel NL	6	B2	Roquefort F	30	C2	St-Amans F	33	D2
Revel F	39	D3	Roquefort-			St-Amant-		
Révigny F	21	F2	sur-Soulzon F	39	E4	Roche-Savine F	33	E4
Revin F	13	F3	Rosans F	34	B1	St-Ambroix F	33	E1
Rhede D	7	E3	Roscoff F	8	C3	St-Amé F	22	C2
Rheinau D	23	E3	Rosporden F	8	B1	St-Amour F	28	B2
Rheinbach D	15	D3	Rostassac F	31	F2	St-André F	11	E1
Rheinberg D	7	D2	Rostrenen F	8	C1	St-André-de-Cubzac F	30	C4
Rheinböllen D	15	E2	Rothéneuf F	9	F2	St-André-les-Alpes F	42	B3
Rheindahlen D	7	D1	Rotterdam NL	6	B3	St Annaparochie NL	3	D4
Rheine D	7	F3	Rottweil D	23	F2	St-Anthème F	33	E4
Rheinfelden CH	29	F4	Roubaix F	5	D1	St-Antonin-		
Rheinfelden D	29	F4	Rouen F	11	E2	Noble-Val F	32	A1
Rheinzabern D	23	F4	Rouffach F	23	D1	St-Aubin-d'Aubigné F	9	F1
Rhenen NL	6	C3	Rougé F	17	F3	St-Aubin-		
Rhens D	15	E3	Rougemont F	29	D4	du-Cormier F	17	F4
Rheydt D	7	D1	Rougemont F	29	E4	St-Aubin-sur-Mer F	10	C3
Rhinau F	23	E2	Rouillac F	24	C2	St-Aulaye F	31	D4
Rhynern D	7	F2	Roujan F	39	F3	St-Avold F	22	C4
Riaillé F	17	F3	Roulers			St-Aygulf F	42	B2
Rians F	41	E3	(Roeselare) B	5	D2	St-Bard F	26	B1
Ribeauville F	23	D2	Roussillon F	41	D3	St-Béat F	38	A3
Ribécourt F	12	C2	Rouvres-			St-Beauzély F	32	C1
Ribemont F	13	D3	en-Xaintois F	22	B2	St-Benin F	27	D3
Ribérac F	31	E4	Royan F	24	A2	St-Benoît F	25	F3
Ribes de Freser E	38	C1	Royat F	26	C1	St-Benoît-sur-Loire F	20	A2
Richelieu F	18	C1	Roybon F	34	B3	St-Bertrand-		
Riegel D	23	E2	Roye F	12	C3	de-Comminges F	37	F2
Rieumes F	38	B3	Royère-			St Blasien D	23	E1
Rieupeyroux F	32	B2	de-Vassivière F	26	A1	St-Blin F	22	A2
Rieux F	38	B3	Rozay-en-Brie F	20	C4	St-Bonnet F	34	C1
Riez F	41	F3	Rozoy F	13	E2	St-Bonnet-de-Joux F	27	E2
Rignac F	32	B2	Rüdesheim D	15	F2	St-Bonnet-		
Rijssen NL	3	D1	Rue F	12	B4	le-Château F	33	E3
Rillé F	18	C2	Ruelle-sur-Touvre F	24	C2	St-Brevin-les-Pins F	17	D2
Riom F	26	C1	Ruffec F	25	D2	St-Brice-en-Coglès F	10	A1
Riom-			Ruffieux F	34	C4	St-Brieuc F	9	D2
ès-Montagnes F	32	C3	Rugles F	11	E1	St-Calais F	19	D3
Rioz F	28	C4	Rülzheim D	23	F4	St-Cast-le-Guildo F	9	E2
Ripoll E	38	C1	Rumigny F	13	E2	St-Céré F	32	B3
Riquewihr F	23	D2	Rumilly F	35	D4	St-Cergue CH	28	C2
Riscle F	37	E3	Rupt F	22	C1	St-Cernin F	32	C3
Riva-Bella F	10	C3	Rust D	23	E2	St-Chamas F	41	D3
Rivarolo Canavese I	35	F2	Ruswil CH	29	F2	St-Chamond F	34	A3
Rive-de-Gier F	34	A3	Rutenbrock D	3	F2	St-Chély-d'Apcher F	33	D2
Rivesaltes F	39	E2	Ruurlo NL	7	D3	St-Chély-d'Aubrac F	32	C2
Rivoli I	35	F2	Ruwer D	15	D2	St-Chinian F	39	E3
Roanne F	27	E1	Rye GB	4	A2	St-Ciers F	24	B1
Rocamadour F	32	A3	Rysum D	3	F4	St-Clar F	31	E1
Rochechouart F	25	D2				St-Claud F	25	D2
Rochefort F	24	B2				St-Claude F	28	C1
Rochefort B	14	B3	**S**			St-Cyprien F	31	E3
Rochefort-en-Terre F	17	D1				St-Cyprien-Plage F	39	E1
Rochefort-s-Nenon F	28	B3				St-Denis F	12	B1
Rochehaut B	14	A2	's Heerenberg NL	7	D3	St-Denis d'Orques F	18	C3
Rochemaure F	34	A1	's-Hertogen-Bosch NL	6	C3	St-Denis-d'Oléron F	24	A3
Rocheservière F	17	E2	Saales F	23	D2	St-Didier-en-Velay F	33	F3
Rochester GB	4	A3	Saanen CH	29	E1	St-Dié F	23	D2
Rockenhausen D	15	E1	Saarbrücken D	23	D4	St-Dizier F	21	F3
Rocroi F	13	F3	Saarburg D	15	D1	St-Donat-		
Roden NL	3	E3	Saarlouis D	15	D1	sur-l'Herbasse F	34	B2
Rodez F	32	C2	Sabiñánigo E	37	D1	St-Emilion F	31	D3
Roermond NL	6	C1	Sablé-sur-Sarthe F	18	B3	St-Étienne F	41	E3
Roeselare			Sables-d'Or-les-Pins F	9	E2	St-Étienne F	33	F3
(Roulers) B	5	D2	Sabres F	30	B2	St-Étienne-		
Rogliano F	43	b3	Sadaba E	36	B1	de-Baïgorry F	36	C3
Rognac F	41	D2				St-Étienne-		
Rohan F	9	D1				de-St-Geoirs F	34	B3

St-Étienne-de-Tinée F	42	C4
St-Fargeau F	20	B2
St-Firmin F	34	C2
St-Florent F	43	b3
St-Florent F	18	A2
St-Florent F	26	B4
St-Florentin F	21	D2
St-Flour F	33	D3
St-Galmier F	33	F4
St-Gaudens F	38	A3
St-Gaultier F	25	F3
St-Geniez-d'Olt F	32	C2
St-Genis-		
de-Saintonge F	24	B1
St-Genix-		
sur-Guiers F	34	C3
St Georgen D	23	F1
St-Georges F	18	A2
St-Georges-		
de-Didonne F	24	A2
St-Geours-		
de-Maremne F	30	A1
St-Germain F	25	E1
St-Germain F	12	B1
St-Germain-		
de-Joux F	28	B1
St-Germain-		
des-Vaux F	10	A4
St-Germain-du-Bois F	28	B2
St-Germain-		
du-Plain F	28	A2
St-Germain-l'Herm F	33	E4
St-Germain-Laval F	33	F4
St-Germain-		
Lembron F	33	D4
St-Germain-Plage F	10	A3
St-Gervais F	39	E3
St-Gervais-		
d'Auvergne F	26	C1
St-Gervais-		
les-Bains F	35	E4
St-Géry F	32	A2
St-Gildas-des-Bois F	17	E3
St-Gilles F	40	C3
St-Gilles-		
Croix-de-Vie F	17	D1
St Gingolph CH	29	D1
St-Girons F	38	B3
St-Girons-Plage F	30	A2
St Goar D	15	E2
St Goarshausen D	15	E2
St-Gorgon-Main F	28	C3
St-Guénolé F	8	B1
St Helier GBJ	9	F3
St-Hilaire-		
de-Villefranche F	24	B2
St-Hilaire-		
du-Harcouët F	10	B1
St-Hippolyte F	29	D3
St-Hippolyte-		
du-Fort F	40	B4
St-Honoré F	27	E3
St-Hubert B	14	B3
St-Imier CH	29	E3
St Ingbert D	23	D4
St-Jacut F	9	E2
St-James F	10	A1
St-Jean-Brévelay F	17	D4
St-Jean-Cap-Ferrat F	42	C2
St-Jean-d'Angély F	24	B2
St-Jean-de-Bournay F	34	B3
St-Jean-de-Losne F	28	B3
St-Jean-de-Luz F	36	B3
St-Jean-		
de-Maurienne F	35	D2
St-Jean-de-Monts F	17	D1
St-Jean-du-Bruel F	40	A4
St-Jean-du-Gard F	40	B4
St-Jean-le-Thomas F	10	A2
St-Jean-		
Pied-de-Port F	36	C3
St-Jeoire F	28	C1
St-Jorioz F	35	D4
St-Jory F	38	C4
St-Jouan-de-l'Isle F	9	E1
St-Julien F	38	B3

St-Julien-Chapteuil F 33 E3
St-Julien-
de-Vouvantes F 17 F3
St-Julien-
en-Beauchêne F ...... 34 CI
St-Julien-
en-Genevois F .... 28 CI
St-Julien-l'Ars F 25 D3
St-Junien F 25 E2
St-Just-
en-Chaussée F 12 B2
St-Just-en-Chevalet F ... 27 DI
St-Justin F 30 C2
St-Lary-Soulan F 37 E2
St-Laurent F 25 E2
St-Laurent F 10 C3
St-Laurent-
en-Grandvaux F 28 C2
St-Laurent-Médoc F ... 24 AI
St-Leger F 27 E3
St-Léonard-
de-Noblat F .... 25 EI
St-Lô F 10 B2
St-Louis F 29 F4
St-Loup-
sur-Semouse F .... 22 BI
St-Luc CH .... 29 EI
St-Lunaire F 9 E2
St-Lys F 38 B4
St-Macaire F 30 C3
St-Maclou F 11 D2
St-Maixent-l'Ecole F ... 24 C3
St-Malo F 9 F2
St-Marcellin F 34 B2
St-Mars-la-Jaille F 17 F3
St-Martin-
d'Auxigny F 26 C4
St-Martin-
de-Londres F 40 B3
St-Martin-de-Ré F 24 A3
St-Martin-Vésubie F ... 42 C3
St-Martory F 38 B3
St-Mathieu F .... 25 DI
St-Maurice CH .... 29 DI
St Maurice-
sur-Moselle F .... 22 CI
St-Maximin-
la-Ste-Baume F 41 E2
St-Méen F .... 9 EI
St-Michel-
de-Maurienne F 35 D2
St-Michel-en-Grève F ... 8 C2
St-Michel-
en-l'Herm F 24 A3
St-Mihiel F 22 B4
St-Nazaire F 17 D2
St-Nectaire F 33 D4
St-Nicolas F 17 E3
St Nicolas-de-Port F ... 22 C3
St-Nicolas-
du-Pélem F 9 D2
St-Niklaas B 5 F2
St Niklaus CH .... 29 EI
St Oedenrode NL 6 C2
St-Omer F .... 4 CI
St-Palais F 36 C3
St-Palais-sur-Mer F ... 24 A2
St-Pardoux-
la-Rivière F .... 25 DI
St-Paul F 42 C2
St-Paul F .... 35 DI
St-Paul-Cap-de-Joux F ... 39 D4
St-Paul-
de-Fenouillet F 39 D2
St-Pauliene F 33 E3
St-Pé F 37 E3
St-Péray F 34 A2
St-Père-en-Retz F 17 D2
St Peter Port GBG 9 F4
St-Philbert F 17 E2
St-Pierre-d'Albigny F ... 35 D3
St-Pierre-d'Oléron F ... 24 A3
St-Pierre-
de-Chartreuse F 34 C3
St-Pierre-
de-Chignac F 31 E4

St-Pierre-Église F 10 B4
St-Pierre-
le-Moûtier F 26 C3
St-Pierre-Quiberon F ... 16 C3
St-Pierre-sur-Dives F ... 11 D2
St-Pois F 10 B2
St-Pol-de-Léon F 8 C3
St-Pol-sur-Ternoise F ... 12 C4
St-Pons F 39 E3
St-Porchaire F 24 B2
St-Pourçain F 26 C2
St-Privat F 32 B3
St-Quay-Portrieux F ... 9 D2
St-Quentin F 13 D3
St-Rambert-
d'Albon F 34 B3
St-Rambert-
en-Bugey F 34 C4
St-Raphaël F 42 B2
St-Rémy-
de-Provence F 41 D3
St-Renan F 8 B2
St-Riquier F 12 B4
St-Rome-de-Tarn F ... 39 E4
St-Saëns F 11 F3
St-Satur F .... 20 BI
St-Saulge F 27 D4
St-Sauvant F 25 D3
St-Sauveur-
en-Puisaye F 20 C2
St-Sauveur-
le-Vicomte F 10 B3
St-Sauveur-
sur-Tinée F 42 C3
St-Savin F 30 C4
St-Savin F 25 E3
St-Seine-l'Abbaye F ... 28 A4
St-Sernin-sur-Rance F ... 39 E4
St-Sever F .... 30 BI
St-Sever F 10 B2
St-Symphorien F 30 C3
St-Symphorien-
d'Ozon F 34 B4
St-Symphorien-
de-Lay F .... 27 EI
St-Symphorien-
sur-Coise F 34 A4
St-Thiébault F 22 A2
St-Trivier-
de-Courtes F 28 A2
St-Tropez F 42 B2
St-Truiden B .... 6 BI
St-Vaast-la-Hougue F ... 10 B3
St-Valery-en-Caux F ... 11 E3
St-Valery-
sur-Somme F 12 B4
St-Vallier-de-Thiey F ... 42 B3
St-Vallier-sur-Rhône F ... 34 B3
St-Vaury F 26 A2
St-Véran F .... 35 EI
St Vincent I 35 F3
St-Vincent-
de-Tyrosse F .... 30 AI
St Vith B 14 C3
St-Vivien-de-Médoc F ... 24 AI
St Wendel D .... 15 DI
St-Yrieix-la-Perche F ... 25 EI
Ste-Anne-d'Auray F ... 16 C4
Ste-Anne-la-Palud F ... 8 B2
Ste-Croix CH 29 D2
Ste-Croix-Volvestre F ... 38 B3
Ste-Enimie F .... 33 DI
Ste-Foy-la-Grande F ... 31 D3
Ste-Gauburge-
Ste-Colombe F ...... 11 DI
Ste-Hélène F 30 B4
Ste-Hermine F 24 B4
Ste-Marie-
aux-Mines F 23 D2
Ste-Marie-
de-Campan F 37 E2
Ste-Maure-
de-Touraine F .... 18 CI
Ste-Maxime F 42 B2
Ste-Menehould F 21 F4
Ste-Mère-Église F 10 B3
Ste-Sévère F 26 B3

Ste-Suzanne F 18 B3
Ste-Tulle F 41 E3
Stes-Maries-
de-la-Mer F 40 C3
Sainte-Lucie-
de-Tallano F .... 43 aI
Sainte-Marie-Sicché F ... 43 a2
Saintes F 24 B2
Saissac F 39 D3
Salardú E 38 A2
Salbris F .... 19 FI
Salernes F 42 A2
Salers F 32 C3
Salies-de-Béarn F 37 D3
Salies-du-Salat F 38 B3
Salignac-Eyvigues F ... 31 F3
Salins F 28 C3
Sallanches F 35 E4
Sallent de Gállego F ... 37 D2
Salles F 30 B3
Salles F 38 C3
Salles-Curan F .... 32 CI
Salon F 21 D3
Salon-de-Provence F ... 41 D3
Salses-le-Château F ... 39 E2
Saluzzo I .... 35 FI
Salvatierra E 36 A3
Salviac F 31 F3
Samadet F 37 D4
Samatan F 38 B4
Samer F .... 4 BI
Samitier E .... 37 EI
Samoëns F 35 E4
San Anton Leitza E ... 36 B3
San Martín de Unx E ... 36 B2
San Remo I 43 D3
San Sebastián/
Donostia E 36 B3
Sanary-sur-Mer F 41 E2
Sancergues F 26 C4
Sancerre F .... 20 BI
Sancoins F 26 C3
Sandwich GB 4 B3
Sangüesa E 36 B2
Sanguinet F 30 B3
Sannenmöser CH ...... 29 EI
Sant Julià
de Lória AND .... 38 BI
Santa Cruz
de Campezo E 36 A2
Santa Joan
de les Abadesses E... 39 DI
Santa Margherita
Ligure I 43 F3
Santa Severa F 43 b3
Santena I 35 F2
Santesteban E 36 B3
Sappemeer NL 3 E3
Saqués E 37 D2
Saramon F 38 B4
Sarlat-la-Canéda F ... 31 F3
Sarralbe F 23 D4
Sarre-Union F 23 D3
Sarrebourg F 23 D3
Sarreguemines F 23 D4
Sarron F 37 E3
Sartène F .... 43 aI
Sartilly F 10 A2
Sarzeau F 17 D3
Sassenage F 34 C2
Sassenheim NL 2 B2
Saucats F 30 C3
Saugues F 33 D3
Saujon F 24 B2
Saulieu F 27 E4
Sault F 41 E4
Saulx F .... 22 BI
Saulxures F .... 22 CI
Saumur F 18 B2
Sauve F 40 B4
Sauveterre-
de-Béarn F 36 C3
Sauveterre-de-
Guyenne F 31 D3
Sauxillanges F 33 D4
Sauze d'Oulx I 35 E2
Sauzé-Vaussais F 24 C2

Sauzon F 16 C3
Savenay F 17 E3
Saverdun F 38 C3
Saverne F 23 D3
Savigliano I .... 35 FI
Savignac-les-Eglises F ... 31 E4
Savigny-sur-Braye F ... 19 D3
Savines-le-Lac F ...... 35 DI
Savona I 43 E3
Scaër F .... 8 CI
Schaffhausen CH ...... 23 FI
Schagen NL 2 B3
Schermbeck D 7 E2
Scheveningen NL ...... 2 AI
Schiermonnikoog NL ... 3 D4
Schifferstadt D 23 F4
Schilde B 6 A2
Schiltach D 23 F2
Schirmeck F 23 D2
Schlangenbad D 15 F2
Schleiden D 15 D3
Schluchsee D .... 23 EI
Schönau D 29 F4
Schönecken D 15 D3
Schönwald D .... 23 EI
Schoondijke NL 5 E2
Schoonebeek NL 3 E2
Schoonhoven NL 6 B3
Schoonoord NL 3 E2
Schopfheim D 29 F4
Schramberg D 23 F2
Schüpfheim CH 29 F2
Schüttorf D 7 F4
Schwarzsee CH 29 E2
Schweich D 15 D2
Schwelm D .... 7 EI
Schwenningen D ...... 23 FI
Schwerte D 7 F2
Schwetzingen D 23 F4
Seclin F 13 D4
Secondigny F 24 C4
Sedan F 14 A2
Séderon F 41 E4
Seelbach D 23 E2
Sées F .... 11 DI
Segonzac F 24 C2
Segré F 18 A3
Seiches-sur-le-Loir F ... 18 B2
Seilhac F 32 B4
Seira E .... 37 EI
Sélestat F 23 D2
Selles F .... 19 EI
Sellières F 28 B2
Selm D 7 F2
Selongey F .... 21 FI
Seltz F 23 E3
Semur-en-Auxois F ... 21 DI
Sénas F 41 D3
Senden D 7 F3
Sendenhorst D 7 F2
Senlis F 12 C2
Sennecey-le-Grand F ... 28 A2
Senonches F 19 E4
Senones F 23 D2
Sens F 20 C3
Sept-Saulx F .... 13 EI
Seraing B 14 B4
Sérent F 17 D4
Sermaize-les-Bains F ... 21 F3
Serres F .... 34 CI
Serrières F 34 A3
Sesma E 36 A2
Sestriere I 35 E2
Sète F 40 B3
Settimo Torinese I 35 F2
Seurre F 28 B3
Sévérac-le-Château F ... 32 CI
Sevrier F 35 D4
Seyches F 31 D3
Seyne F 42 B4
Seyssel F 34 C4
Sézanne F 21 D4
Sheerness GB 4 A3
Siddeburen NL 3 E3
Siegburg D 15 E4
Siegen D 15 F4
Sierck-les-Bains F ...... 14 CI

Sierentz F. 29 E4
Sierre CH. 29 E1
Sigean F 39 E2
Signy-l'Abbaye F 13 E2
Sillé-le-Guillaume F 18 C4
Simmerath D 14 C4
Simmern D 15 E2
Simplon CH. 29 F1
Singen D 23 F1
Sinzig D 15 E3
Sion CH 29 E1
Siorac-en-Périgord F. 31 E3
Sissach CH. 29 F3
Sisteron F 41 F4
Sittard NL 6 C1
Sittingbourne GB 4 A3
Six-Fours-les-Plages F.. .... 41 E1
Sizun F 8 B2
Sliedrecht NL 6 B3
Sloten NL. 2 C3
Sluis NL. 5 E2
Sluis NL. 5 F3
Smilde NL 3 E3
Sneek NL 3 D3
Soest NL 6 C4
Soestdijk NL 2 C1
Sögel D 3 F2
Soignies B 13 E4
Soissons F 13 D2
Soldeu AND 38 C2
Solenzara F 43 b1
Solingen D 7 E1
Solliès-Pont F 41 E2
Solothurn CH. 29 E3
Sombernon F 28 A4
Sommesous F 21 E4
Sommières F 40 B3
Sonceboz CH 29 E3
Sonsbeck D 7 D2
Sopeira E 38 A1
Sore F 30 C2
Sort E 38 B1
Sos del Rey
  Católico E 36 C2
Sospel F 42 C3
Sotta F 43 b1
Souesmes F 19 F1
Soufflenheim F 23 E3
Souillac F 32 A3
Souilly F 22 A4
Soulac-sur-Mer F 24 A2
Soulaines-Dhuys F 21 E3
Soultz F 23 D1
Soultz F 23 E3
Soumoulou F 37 E2
Souppes-sur-Loing F 20 B3
Sourdeval F 10 B2
Sousceyrac F 32 B3
Soustons F 30 A2
Southend-on-Sea GB. 4 A3
Souvigny F 26 C2
Spa B 14 C3
Spaichingen D 23 F1
Spakenburg NL 2 C1
Speyer D 23 F4
Spiez CH 29 E2
Spijkenisse NL 6 A3
Spincourt F 14 B1
Stadskanaal NL 3 E3
Stadtkyll D 15 D3
Stadtlohn D 7 E3
Stainville F 21 F3
Stalden CH 29 F1
Stavelot B 14 C3
Stavenisse NL 5 F3
Staveren NL 2 C3
Stechelberg CH 29 F1
Steenbergen NL 6 A3
Steenvoorde F 4 C3
Steenwijk NL 3 D2
Steinfurt D 7 F3
Stellendam NL 5 F3
Stenay F 14 A2
Stiens NL 3 D4
Stolberg D 14 C4
Straelen D 7 D2
Strasbourg F 23 E3

Stromberg D 15 E2
Stühlingen D 23 F1
Süchteln D 7 D2
Sudbury GB 4 A4
Suippes F 13 E1
Sully-sur-Loire F 20 A2
Sulz D 23 F2
Sumiswald CH. 29 F2
Sundern D 7 F1
Surgères F 24 B3
Sursee CH 29 F3
Survilliers F 12 B1
Susa I 35 E2
Swalmen NL 6 C2

T

Tafalla E 36 B2
Taggia I 43 D3
Tain-l'Hermitage F 34 B2
Taizé F 27 F2
Tallard F 34 C1
Talloires F 35 D4
Talmont F 24 B2
Talmont-St-Hilaire F 24 A4
Tancarville F 11 E3
Taninges F 35 E4
Tarare F 34 A4
Tarascon F 40 C3
Tarascon-
  sur-Ariège F 38 C2
Tarbes F 37 E3
Tardets-Sorholus F 36 C3
Tarnos F 36 C4
Tartas F 30 B2
Taunusstein D 15 F2
Tauves F 32 C4
Tavannes CH. 29 E3
Tavaux F 28 B3
Tavernes F 41 F2
Tecklenburg D 7 F3
Tegelen NL 7 D2
Telgte D 7 F3
Temse B 5 F2
Tence F 33 F3
Tende F 43 D3
Tenterden GB 4 A2
Ter Apel NL 3 E2
Terneuzen NL 5 E2
Terrasson-
  la-Villedieu F 31 F3
Tervuren B 6 A1
Tessy-sur-Vire F 10 B2
Thalfang D 15 D2
Thann F 23 D1
Thénezay F 25 D4
Thenon F 31 F4
Théoule F 42 B2
Thérouanne F 4 C1
Theux B 14 C4
Thiaucourt-
  Regniéville F 22 B4
Thiberville F 11 D2
Thiélbemont-
  Farémont F 21 E3
Thiers F 27 D1
Thionville F 14 C1
Thivars F 19 E4
Thiviers F 31 E4
Thizy F 27 E1
Thoissey F 27 F1
Tholey D 15 D1
Thonon F 28 C1
Thouarcé F 18 B2
Thouars F 18 B1
Thueyts F 33 E2
Thuir F 39 D1
Thun CH 29 E2
Thury-Harcourt F 10 C2
Tiel NL 6 C3
Tielt B 5 E2
Tienen B 6 B1
Tiercé F 18 B3

Tignes F 35 E3
Til-Châtel F 28 B4
Tilburg NL 6 B2
Tinchebray F 10 B2
Titisee D 23 E1
Titz D 7 D1
Todtmoos D 29 F4
Todtnau D 23 E1
Tolosa E 36 A3
Tongeren (Tongres) B.. .... 14 B4
Tongres (Tongeren) B.. .... 14 B4
Tonnay-Boutonne F 24 B2
Tonnay-Charente F 24 B2
Tonneins F 31 D2
Tonnerre F 21 D2
Torhout B 5 D2
Torigni-sur-Vire F 10 B2
Torino I 35 F2
Torla E 37 D1
Torre Pellice I 35 E1
Torriglia I 43 F4
Tôtes F 11 F3
Toucy F 20 C2
Toul F 22 B3
Toulon F 41 E2
Toulon-sur-Arroux F 27 E3
Toulouse F 38 C4
Tourcoing F 5 D1
Tournai (Doornik) B.. .... 13 D4
Tournan F 20 B4
Tournay F 37 E2
Tournon F 34 A2
Tournon-d'Agenais F 31 E2
Tournon-St-Martin F 25 E3
Tournus F 28 A2
Tours F 19 D2
Toury F 19 F3
Traben-Trarbach D 15 D2
Tramelan CH 29 E3
Trassem D 14 C1
Travers CH 29 D2
Trébeurden F 8 C3
Tréboul F 8 B2
Trégastel F 8 C3
Tréguier F 9 D2
Treignac F 32 B4
Treis D 15 E3
Tremp E 38 A1
Trets F 41 E2
Trévoux F 27 F1
Triaize F 24 B3
Triaucourt-
  en-Argonne F 21 F4
Triberg D 23 E2
Trie F 37 F3
Trier D 15 D2
Trittenheim D 15 D2
Troarn F 10 C2
Trois-Ponts B 14 C3
Trouville F 11 D3
Troyes F 21 D3
Truchtersheim F 23 E3
Trun F 11 D2
Tuchan F 39 E2
Tudela E 36 B1
Tuffé F 19 D3
Tulle F 32 B4
Tullins F 34 C3
Turckheim F 23 D2
Turnhout B 6 B2
Tuttlingen D 23 F1
Twist D 3 E2
Tzummarum NL 2 C3

U

Uckange F 14 C1
Uden NL 6 C3
Uelsen D 3 E2
Ugine F 35 D3
Uithoorn NL 2 B2
Uithuizen NL 3 E4
Ulmen D 15 D3

Unna D 7 F2
Urdos F 37 D2
Uriage-les-Bains F 34 C2
Urk NL 2 C2
Ury F 20 B3
Ussel F 32 C4
Ustaritz F 36 C3
Utrecht NL 6 B3
Uzel F 9 D1
Uzerche F 32 B4
Uzès F 40 C4

V

Vaas F 18 C2
Vaassen NL 3 D1
Vado Ligure I 43 E3
Vaiges F 18 B3
Vailly F 20 B1
Vailly F 13 D2
Vaison-la-Romaine F 41 D4
Val d'Esquières F. 42 B2
Val d'Isère F 35 E3
Val Thorens F 35 D2
Val-Claret F 35 E3
Val-Suzon F 28 A4
Valberg F 42 B3
Valbonnais F 34 C2
Valcarlos E 36 C3
Valdahon F 28 C3
Valençay F 19 E1
Valence F 31 E2
Valence F 34 B2
Valence d'Albigeois F 32 B1
Valence-Sur Baise F. 31 D1
Valenciennes F 13 D4
Valensole F 41 F3
Valkenburg NL 6 C1
Valkenswaard NL 6 C2
Valleraugue F 40 B4
Vallet F 17 F2
Valloire F 35 D2
Vallon-en-Sully F 26 B3
Vallon-Pont-d'Arc F 33 F1
Vallorbe F 28 C2
Vallorcine F 35 E4
Vallouise F 35 D2
Valmorel F 35 D3
Valognes F 10 B3
Valras-Plage F 39 F2
Valréas F 34 B1
Vals-les-Bains F 33 F2
Valtierra E 36 B1
Valtournenche I 35 F3
Vannes F 17 D3
Varades F 18 A2
Varazze I 43 E4
Varces F 34 C2
Varengeville-
  sur-Mer F 11 F3
Varennes-
  en-Argonne F 14 A1
Varennes-sur-Allier F 27 D2
Varilhes F 38 C3
Vars F 35 D1
Varsseveld NL 7 D3
Varzy F 27 D4
Vassy F 10 C2
Vatan F 26 B4
Vaucouleurs F 22 B3
Vauvert F 40 C3
Vauville F 10 A4
Vauvillers F 22 B1
Vayrac F 32 B3
Veendam NL 3 E3
Veenendaal NL 6 C3
Veere NL 5 E3
Veghel NL 6 C2
Velbert D 7 E2
Veldhoven NL 6 C2
Velp NL 7 D3
Venaco F 43 b2
Vence F 42 C3

Vendeuvre F 21 E2
Vendôme F 19 D2
Venlo NL 7 D2
Venray NL 6 C2
Ventimíglia I 43 D3
Vera de Bidasoa E 36 B3
Verberie F 12 C2
Verbier CH 35 F4
Verdun F 22 A4
Verfeil F 38 C4
Vergt F 31 E3
Vermenton F 20 C1
Vernet F 38 C3
Vernet-les-Bains F 39 D1
Verneuil F 11 E1
Vernon F 11 F2
Verny F 22 C4
Verrès I 35 F3
Verrières-de-Joux F 29 D2
Versailles F 12 B1
Versoix CH 28 C1
Verteillac F 24 C1
Vertus F 21 D4
Verviers B 14 C4
Vervins F 13 E2
Verzuolo I 35 F1
Verzy F 13 E1
Vesoul F 28 C4
Veules-les-Roses F 11 E3
Veulettes-sur-Mer F 11 E3
Veurne (Furnes) B 5 D2
Vevey CH 29 D1
Veynes F 34 C1
Veyrier F 35 D4
Vézelay F 20 C1
Vézelise F 22 B3
Vézénobres F 40 C4
Viais F 17 E2
Vianden L 14 C2
Vianen NL 6 B3
Vianne F 31 D2
Vias F 40 A3
Vibraye F 19 D3
Vic F 33 D4
Vic-en-Bigorre F 37 E3
Vic-Fezensac F 37 F4
Vic-sur-Aisne F 12 C2
Vic-sur-Cère F 32 C3
Vicdessos F 38 B2
Vichy F 27 D2
Vico F 43 a2
Vidauban F 42 A2
Vielha E 38 A2
Vielsalm B 14 C3
Vienne F 34 B3
Viersen D 7 D2
Vierzon F 19 F1
Vieux-Boucau-
   les-Bains F 30 A2
Vif F 34 C2
Vigneulles F 22 B4
Vignory F 21 F2
Vihiers F 18 B2
Villaines-la-Juhel F 18 C4
Villandraut F 30 C3
Villandry F 18 C2
Villard-de-Lans F 34 C2
Villars F 42 C3
Villars CH 29 D1
Villars-les-Dombes F 28 A1
Villé F 23 D2
Ville-en-Tardenois F 13 D1
Villebois-Lavalette F 24 C1
Villedieu-les-Poêles F ... 10 B2
Villefagnan F 24 C2
Villefort F 33 E1
Villefranche F 42 C2
Villefranche-
   d'Albigeois F 39 D4
Villefranche-
   de-Lauragais F 38 C3
Villefranche-
   de-Lonchat F 31 D4
Villefranche-
   de-Rouergue F 32 B2
Villefranche-
   du-Périgord F 31 E3

Villefranche-
   sur-Cher F 19 E1
Villefranche-
   sur-Saône F 27 F1
Villemur F 31 F1
Villenauxe-
   la-Grande F 21 D3
Villeneuve F 32 B2
Villeneuve F 41 D4
Villeneuve-de-Berg F ... 33 F1
Villeneuve-
   de-Marsan F 30 C2
Villeneuve-
   l'Archevêque F 20 C3
Villeneuve-Loubet F 42 C2
Villeneuve-
   sur-Allier F 27 D3
Villeneuve-sur-Lot F 31 E2
Villeneuve-
   sur-Yonne F 20 C2
Villeréal F 31 E3
Villers F 11 D3
Villers-Bocage F 10 C2
Villers-Bretonneux F 12 C3
Villers-Cotterêts F 12 C1
Villers-le-Lac F 29 D3
Villers-St-Georges F 20 C4
Villersexel F 29 D4
Villerville F 11 D3
Villingen D 23 F1
Vimoutiers F 11 D2
Vinádio I 42 C4
Vinay F 34 B3
Vinça F 39 D1
Vinon-sur-Verdon F 41 E3
Vire F 10 B2
Virieu F 34 C3
Virieu-le-Grand F 34 C4
Virton B 14 B2
Visé B 14 C4
Visp CH 29 F1
Vitré F 18 A4
Vitry-le-François F 21 E3
Vitteaux F 27 F4
Vittel F 22 B2
Vivario F 43 b2
Viviers F 34 A1
Vivonne F 25 D3
Vizille F 34 C2
Vizzavona F 43 b2
Vlaardingen NL 6 A3
Vlagtwedde NL 3 F3
Vlissingen NL 5 E2
Void F 22 B3
Voiron F 34 C3
Voise F 19 F4
Voix F 41 E3
Volendam NL 2 C2
Völklingen D 23 D4
Voltri I 43 E4
Voorschoten NL 2 B1
Voorst NL 7 D3
Voreppe F 34 C3
Vorey F 33 E3
Vouillé F 25 D4
Vouvray F 19 D2
Vouziers F 13 F1
Voves F 19 E3
Vreden D 7 E3
Vresse B 14 A2
Vron F 12 B4
Vroomshoop NL 3 E2
Vught NL 6 C3

Waltrop D 7 F2
Wangenbourg F 23 D3
Waregem B 5 E1
Waremme B 14 B4
Warnsveld NL 7 D3
Wasselonne F 23 D3
Wassenaar NL 2 A1
Wassenberg D 7 D1
Wasserbillig L 14 C2
Wassy F 21 F3
Waterloo B 13 F4
Waulsort B 14 A3
Wavre B 14 A4
Waxweiler D 14 C3
Weener D 3 F3
Weert NL 6 C2
Weeze D 7 D2
Wegberg D 7 D1
Wehr D 29 F4
Wehr D 15 E3
Weilburg D 15 F3
Well NL 7 D2
Wellin B 14 B3
Wemperhaardt L 14 C3
Wengen CH 29 F1
Wépion B 14 A3
Werbomont B 14 B3
Werdohl D 7 F1
Werl D 7 F2
Werlte D 3 F2
Wermelskirchen D 7 E1
Werne D 7 F2
Wesel D 7 D2
West-Terschelling NL 2 C4
Westende-Bad B 5 D2
Westerholt D 3 F4
Westerlo B 6 B1
Westkapelle NL 5 E3
Wetter D 7 E2
Wetteren B 5 E1
Wettringen D 7 F3
Whitstable GB 4 A3
Wierden NL 3 E2
Wiesbaden D 15 F2
Wijhe NL 3 D2
Wildbad D 23 F3
Wildenrath D 7 D1
Willebroek B 6 A2
Willemstad NL 6 A3
Willisau CH 29 F3
Wilnsdorf D 15 F4
Wiltz L 14 C2
Wimereux F 4 B2
Windeck D 15 E4
Winnweiler D 15 E1
Winschoten NL 3 E3
Winsum NL 3 E4
Winterswijk NL 7 E3
Wipperfürth D 7 E1
Wissant F 4 B2
Wissembourg F 23 E3
Wissen D 15 F4
Witham GB 4 A4
Witten D 7 E2
Wittlich D 15 D2
Woerden NL 6 B4
Woerth F 23 E3
Wolfach D 23 E2
Wolfstein D 15 E1
Wolhusen CH 29 F2
Wolvega NL 3 D3
Woodbridge GB 4 B4
Worb CH 29 E2
Workum NL 2 C3
Wormerveer NL 2 B2
Wormhout F 4 C2
Worms D 15 F1
Wörrstadt D 15 F2
Wörth D 23 F3
Wulfen D 7 E2
Wuppertal D 7 E1
Wuustwezel B 6 A2

Xanten D 7 D2
Xertigny F 22 C2
Xhoffraix B 14 C3

Yenne F 34 C3
Yerville F 11 E3
Yesa E 36 C2
Yport F 11 D3
Ypres (Ieper) B 5 D1
Yssingeaux F 33 E3
Yverdon-
   les-Bains CH 29 D2
Yvetot F 11 E3
Yvoir B 14 A3
Yvoire F 28 C1

Zaandam NL 2 B2
Zaltbommel NL 6 C3
Zandvoort NL 2 B2
Zarautz E 36 A3
Zeebrugge B 5 E2
Zeist NL 6 C3
Zell D 15 E2
Zell D 29 F4
Zelzate B 5 E2
Zerf D 15 D1
Zevenaar NL 7 D3
Zevenbergen NL 6 B3
Zicavo F 43 b2
Zierikzee NL 5 F3
Zijpe NL 5 F3
Zinal CH 29 E1
Zoetermeer NL 6 B4
Zofingen CH 29 F3
Zolder B 6 B1
Zonza F 43 b1
Zoutkamp NL 3 E4
Zubiri E 36 B3
Zuidhorn NL 3 E3
Zuidlaren NL 3 E3
Zülpich D 15 D4
Zumaia E 36 A4
Zumarraga E 36 A3
Zundert NL 6 B2
Zutphen NL 7 D3
Zweibrücken D 23 D4
Zweisimmen CH 29 E2
Zwijndrecht NL 6 B3
Zwolle NL 3 D2

Waalwijk NL 6 B3
Wageningen NL 6 C3
Waldbröl D 15 E4
Waldfischbach D 23 E4
Waldkirch D 23 E2
Walton-
   on-the-Naze GB 4 B4